# The Future Agenda

# The Future Agenda

A
Festschrift
in honour of

## John Templeton

on his 80th Birthday
November 29th 1992

*Edited by*

Wilbert Forker

THE HANOVER PRESS
EDINBURGH
SCOTLAND

Published by
The Hanover Press
56 Hanover Street
Edinburgh EH2 2DX

First published 1992
ISBN 0 7073 0723 6

**British Library Cataloguing in Publication Data**

A Catalogue record of this book is available from the
British Library

Typeset by Trinity Typesetting, Edinburgh
Printed in Great Britain

# CONTENTS

|  | Page |
|---|---|
| **Foreward** | vii |
| His Royal Highness, The Duke of Edinburgh KG | |
| **Preface** | viii |
| **Chapter One** | 1 |
| Christian Evangelism at the threshold of the Third Millennium | |
| Reverend Dr Billy Graham | |
| **Chapter Two** | 16 |
| The Bible in the Twenty-First Century — Confronting the Next Frontier | |
| Dr David Burke, Dr Peter Wosh, Ms Laura Goostree | |
| **Chapter Three** | 39 |
| Christian Theology and Scientific Culture: The way ahead | |
| The Very Reverend Professor T. F. Torrance | |
| **Chapter Four** | 54 |
| The Interfaith Movement: The next twenty years | |
| Sir Sigmund Sternberg | |
| **Chapter Five** | 63 |
| Education for a world of accelerating change | |
| The Rt. Hon. Lord Thurlow | |
| **Chapter Six** | 83 |
| Education for World Citizenship | |
| Dr Uwe Kitzinger | |

**Chapter Seven**                                    98

The Future of Theological Education
Dr Thomas Gillespie

**Chapter Eight**                                    114

To save the Earth
Professor Charles Birch

**Chapter Nine**                                     133

The challenge to business in the 1990s
Mr William E. Simon

**Chapter Ten**                                      149

World poverty, trade and trickle down
Reverend Dr Charles Elliott

**Postscript**                                       166

To everything there is a season
Mr John Train

**Contributors**                                     188

29 November 1992

Dear Sir John,

The world is full of experts and specialists, but it is given to few to be pluralists; those exceptional people who not only comprehend the great issues, but whose questing minds can go straight to the heart of the matter. Your highly successful business career and the wide scope of your interests bear witness to both the clarity and originality of your thoughts. You have backed this up with a truly magnificent generosity to the many causes close to your heart.

It is not the passionate revolutionaries who improve the world; the only genuine progress is made by those who have a clearer vision and a greater ability to see through the tangled web of humbug and convention. Your great contribution to human civilisation has been to encourage people to concentrate on the things that really matter and to appraise both conventional as well as unconventional ideas for their true worth.

No one person can change the world by themselves, but each one of us can strive to leave the world a slightly better place. Many do strive, but in your long life you have succeeded in making this world a better place both for present and future generations.

Yours sincerely
Philip

# PREFACE

It is not often in our lifetime that the opportunity comes our way to edit a Festschrift in honour of someone you have known for over twenty years especially when that person is Sir John Templeton.

I first got to know Sir John when I was living in Geneva, Switzerland. He had come to talk about his idea of founding a prize for Progress in Religion, a subject very close to his heart and ever since those days in the late 1970 and early in 1971 we have promoted the idea together.

At the same time Sir John has developed other ideas among which are the firm of Templeton, Galbraith and Hansberger; Templeton College, Oxford and Templeton Theological Seminary, Nassau, The Bahamas. These various activities show part of the wide range of interests that Sir John has had over the years and the writings in the Festschrift take on those themes which have been written by contributors who have been successful in their given disciplines and who have, like Sir John, an eye on the future.

I hope the publishing of this Festschrift will on this very happy occasion of Sir John's 80th birthday be not just a good read but an occasion to look forward with him and with the authors and trust that the world of tomorrow may be an even better place than it is today.

Wilbert Forker
Lyford Cay
The Bahamas
20th July 1992

# 1

## CHRISTIAN EVANGELISM AT THE THRESHOLD OF THE THIRD MILLENNIUM

### BILLY GRAHAM

During the historic World Congress on Evangelism in 1966, Korean pastor Dr Han Kyung-Chik — recipient of the 1992 Templeton Prize for Progress in Religion — challenged the delegates gathered in Berlin's Kongresshalle with these words: 'Surely it is time for us Christians to have a world-wide missionary vision and strategy, not only because the Gospel is for the whole world but also because the world is becoming smaller and smaller, and because the forces of evil are bolder and more rampant.'

Today Dr Han's words ring out to us with even greater relevance and urgency. We stand only a few years away from the end of one millennium and the start of a new. Never has the Christian Church faced so many challenges on so many fronts — political, social, demographic, economic, philosophical. We live in a complex and constantly-shifting world, a world where phrases like 'rapid change' or 'revolutionary developments' have become almost trite and outworn. In the eyes of many, religion has lost its relevance and is little more than a quaint relic from another time.

In response to these challenges the Church today often seems paralysed and confused, battered by the indifference and 'isms' of our age and torn by division and uncertainty. Instead of becoming salt and light, penetrating the spiritual corruption and darkness and alienation of our world with the transforming message of the Gospel, we have been content to withdraw into our separate ecclesiastical ghettos, preoccupied with our own internal affairs and unconcerned about the deepest needs of those around us.

And yet if the challenges are unprecedented, so also are the opportunities. In spite of the difficulties, the 21st Century could mark the greatest evangelistic advance in the history of the Christian Church. In order for this to happen, however, the Church of Jesus Christ (in all of its diversity) must come to grips with the challenges it faces, and must mobilise every possible spiritual and physical resource to declare the Gospel which has been committed to us.

### The Challenges of a New Century

No one knows the future, of course, except God (and the Christian takes comfort in that truth). Nevertheless, we can say with virtual certainty that the years leading up to 2000 and beyond will hold special challenges and barriers for the work of Christian evangelism. Some of these, no doubt, will turn out to be unforeseen surprises and unexpected developments. However, some will be the outworking of present trends, and these deserve careful thought and prayer today if the Church is to respond and do its work effectively. At least four trends in particular will pose a special challenge to Christian evangelism.

### 1. Massive demographic shifts

When the 21st Century dawns the world's population is expected to total a staggering six billion people. That is approximately three times the number of people living just a century before, at the dawn of the 20th Century. By the year 2000 at least half of those people will be living in large cities — uprooted from their past, mobile, often struggling for survival in the midst of extreme poverty, and potentially explosive politically because their dreams may have ended in disillusionment and despair. Already over 50 per cent of the world's population is under twenty-five years of age, and in some countries (particularly in the poorer parts of the world) that number is much higher. Reaching this burgeoning world population with the message of the Gospel will demand new priorities, new approaches, new strategies, and new resources.

## 2. Unrelenting aggressive secularism in many parts of the world

Surely one of the most discouraging historical trends over the last century or so has been the 'de-Christianisation' of many former Christian strongholds (particularly in Europe) because of the massive onslaught of secularism. Secularism, however, has an increasing impact in other parts of the world, such as Japan and other parts of Asia. Nor can we assume that most people living in the former communist nations of Europe will necessarily abandon their secular outlook, even if they have jettisoned its Marxist trappings.

Secularism can take many attitudes toward religion, running the gamut from total indifference to virulent hostility. At its root, however, secularism always excludes God from the world and from daily human life, and the secularist lives for the present without any reference to God or divine moral and spiritual absolutes. A recent poll by George Gallup for the Princeton Religion Research Center revealed that 69 per cent of American adults believe there are few moral absolutes and that what is right or wrong will depend on the situation. (PRC Emerging Trends, February, 1992, p. 3). People with a secular outlook on life often feel very little need of religion, and therefore are indifferent or not open to the Christian message.

## 3. Resurgent non-Christian religions and philosophies

While secularism is growing in some parts of the world, other parts are experiencing a profound religious renaissance. One reason is a growing suspicion that secularism has failed to provide real answers to life's ultimate questions. In commenting on this Professor Diogenes Allen of Princeton Seminary has stated, 'There is an increasing recognition that evil is real and that it cannot be removed merely by education and social reform.' (Quoted in Christianity Today, December 16, 1991, p. 45).

As a result some non-Christian religions (such as some forms of Islam) have grown increasingly suspicious of Western secular trends, believing they could sound the death knell of their religious traditions. In many instances they have grown increasingly militant and aggressive, and some nations which have officially adopted one of these as their sole religion have closed their borders to any Christian influence or activity. The resurgence of non-Christian religions and its impact on the future of Christian evangelism should not be underestimated.

Even in countries like the United States there has been an upsurge in religious interest. In our own work we have discovered in recent years that over half of those who make commitments to Christ are below the age of 25. Not all of the interest, however, has been in historic Christianity; cults and non-western religious traditions have also experienced growth.

It needs to be remembered that over two-thirds of the world's population are not Christian (even in a nominal sense). Vast sections of the non-Christian world have little effective Christian presence in their midst, and many of those are now closed to traditional forms of Christian evangelism, or even Christian-supported social and medical work.

### 4. *Shifting frontiers and emerging fields*
A hundred years from now the last decade of the 20th Century will still be remembered by historians as one of the watershed periods of the modern era. The collapse of Marxism in Eastern Europe and the old Soviet Union has brought about staggering changes, the full impact of which we cannot fully assess as yet.

From the standpoint of Christian evangelism, however, it marks the greatest opening for the furtherance of the Gospel in the history of the Church. Never before has such a vast area, encompassing hundreds of millions of people, opened so suddenly and thoroughly to evangelistic activity. In most of these areas a remnant of the Church has survived the fierce onslaughts of atheism, but the task of evangelising their lands cannot be done by them alone. It will not be easy, and those from outside must learn to temper their enthusiasm with prayer, strategic thinking, cultural sensitivity, and willingness to work as partners with those who are already there. Nevertheless the events of the last few years have presented the Church with an unprecedented and historic opportunity to fill the enormous spiritual and moral vacuum left by atheism with the good news of God's love in Jesus Christ.

What other new fields will emerge in coming decades? For example, will political changes in China — that complex country where almost one out of four of the world's population lives — mean the door will open once again to Christian evangelism from other parts of the world? No one knows the answer to that question. Even if major political changes do take place, they do not necessarily mean China will be open to spiritual influences from other cultures. China has a long and rich cultural heritage, and it has always been suspicious of outside influences and ideas. New strategies and new approaches almost certainly would have to be developed. However, as political and economic changes accelerate in China and elsewhere, we should not be surprised if new and unexpected opportunities suddenly emerge for the work of Christian evangelism in the 21st Century.

As a footnote, however, the 21st Century may also be a time of closing doors and increasing religious polarisation in some parts of the world. It may also be a time when nations which have historically been Christian not only abandon their Christian roots completely (as has already happened in some parts of Europe), but increasingly become the targets of aggressive proselytising by non-Christian cults and religions.

### Those Things Which Do Not Change

In the midst of so many changes in the world — changes so rapid it seems sometimes we can hardly keep up with them, let alone react intelligently to them — it is the unique function of the Church to declare by word and deed that there are some things which never change. This is our message to a world which yearns for peace in the midst of chaos and lives that cry out for stability in the midst of insecurity.

What is that message? It is the message that God — the supreme, unchanging, omnipotent Creator of the universe — loves humanity and wants us to know Him in a personal way. It is the message that humankind has strayed from God and rebelled against Him and His revealed will, and as a result of his sin is alienated from God and from others. It is the message that God has taken the initiative to bridge the gap between God and sinful humanity, and He did this by coming down to earth in the person of Jesus Christ. Through the mystery of the incarnation and the redemptive death of Christ on the cross, we can be forgiven and restored and changed. It is the message that there is hope for the future, because Christ rose from the dead and will reign victorious over all the forces of evil and death and hell.

No, God has not changed, nor has the nature of the human heart changed. Neither has God's message of salvation in Christ changed. And that is why the Gospel is relevant to every individual in every culture, because beneath all the cultural, ethnic, social, economic and political differences which separate us, the deepest needs and hurts and fears of the human heart are still the same. The Gospel is still (in the words of the Apostle Paul) 'the power of God for the salvation of everyone who believes' (Romans 1: 16).

But there is one other thing which has not changed — and that is the commission of Christ to His Church to 'Go into all the world and preach the good news to all creation' (Mark 16: 15).

That command — thoroughly undergirded by a deep love for Christ and for others — impelled the early Christians to go from one end of the Roman Empire to the other, often paying the price for their commitment with their lives. It is that same command which sent Augustine to England, Patrick to Ireland, and Columba to Scotland. In obedience to that same command a host of missionaries and evangelists across the centuries have brought the message of God's love in Christ to the farthest corners of human civilisation. By word and deed they have declared and demonstrated that the Christian message can bring lasting change and hope to the human heart and to the human condition.

No less important, that command also has inspired and challenged a much larger host of individuals who have supported the evangelistic and missionary enterprise by their prayers and financial sacrifice, and who have sought in their own ways to share Christ with their neighbours and friends. That same command and that same love will inspire and challenge a new generation of Christians in the decades to come. 'For Christ's love compels us . . . . We are therefore Christ's ambassadors, as though God were making his appeal through us. We implore you on Christ's behalf: Be reconciled to God' (2 Corinthians 5: 14, 20).

### Some Keys to Effective Evangelism in the 21st Century

Will the Church of Jesus Christ meet the challenge of a new century, with all of its complexity and even confusion? Or will Christians retreat slowly but inexorably into steadily-shrinking ecclesiastical ghettos, their message unheeded and their efforts feeble and ineffective? Now is the time for the Church to come to grips honestly with that question.

What will it take for the evangelistic imperative God has given to His Church to be lived out in the future, so that the 21st Century becomes in reality what it could be — the greatest century for Christian evangelism in history? Let me suggest four keys to effective evangelism — basic principles in evangelism which have always been valid, but which take on special urgency as we approach the challenges of the modern world.

1. *A rediscovery of the biblical message in all of its fullness*
Polls repeatedly demonstrate that if people in the Western
world are asked if they believe in God, or in Jesus, or in
Heaven, or in other basic doctrines of the Christian faith,
large numbers will answer 'Yes'. And yet there is little or no
evidence of vital, living faith in their lives. Why? One reason
is because if those same people are asked 'What is a Christian?' they clearly have little or no comprehension of what
the Bible says about that urgent question.

The evangelistic task first of all should send us back to our
Bibles, carefully and prayerfully studying to uncover the
heart of God's message to an unbelieving world. New
Testament scholars in this century (such as C. H. Dodd)
have pointed us again to the essential message of the early
Church — the *kerygma*. While the Gospel must always be put
in a form which can be understood by each new generation,
the essential message — the good news of the Gospel —
does not change. A rediscovery of the Biblical message in all
of its fullness will mean first of all a re-emphasis of those
truths which form the core of the Christian message.

It also will mean a recovery of the biblical priority of
evangelism. Sad to say, evangelism in many churches today
(and for many individual Christians) seems almost an
appendix or footnote — or even an afterthought — to the
normal workings of the congregation or denomination.

But even a casual inspection of the New Testament will
reveal that evangelism was the priority of the early Church.
Christians are called by God to do many things, but a church
which has lost sight of the priority of evangelism has lost
sight of its primary calling under God. This recalls the oft-
quoted comment by Swiss theologian Emil Brunner: 'A
church exists by mission as fire exists by burning.' (Quoted
in S. E. Wirt and K. Beckstrom, eds., *Living Quotations for
Christians*, New York: Harper and Row, 1974, p. 157).

As a footnote, I believe biblical evangelism needs to be
given much greater priority in theological education as well
— in fact, it should permeate every aspect of a seminary's

curriculum instead of being a minor appendage, as is too often the case. The Scottish theologian James Denney once wrote, 'If evangelists were our theologians or theologians our evangelists, we should at least be nearer the ideal church.' (James Denney, D. D. *The Death of Christ: Its Place and Interpretation in the New Testament.* London: Hodder and Stoughton, 1902, p. viii). A generation of pastors and other church workers inspired with a vision for evangelism and trained to penetrate the world with the Gospel would revolutionize both the Church and the world.

The recovery of the priority of evangelism should not lead us, however, to make a false distinction or dichotomy between the proclamation of the Gospel and social concern. Both are part of God's calling, and both must go hand-in-hand. A Christian who fails to express Christ's love for humanity through compassionate service is not living a life of full discipleship. In like manner, a Christian who fails to express Christ's love for humanity through clear verbal witness also is not living a life of full discipleship. Jesus, we read, 'went through all the towns and villages, teaching in their synagogues, preaching the good news of the kingdom and healing every disease and sickness' (Matthew 9: 35). Immediately afterward He commissioned the twelve disciples to go out and do likewise.

Christians today who have a special interest in evangelism have discovered in new ways the truth of this diversity of ministry. The Lausanne Covenant of 1974 states, 'We affirm that God is both the Creator and the Judge of all men. We therefore should share his concern for justice and reconciliation throughout human society and for the liberation of men from every kind of oppression. . . . The salvation we claim should be transforming us in the totality of our personal and social responsibilities.' (The Lausanne Covenant, Article 5). The Amsterdam Affirmations, a series of fifteen brief principles to which many thousands of evangelists from over 150 nations have subscribed, declares a similar conviction: 'We share Christ's deep concern for the

personal and social sufferings of humanity, and we accept
our responsibility as Christians and as evangelists to do our
utmost to alleviate human need.' (Affirmation XIV).

**2.** *The mobilisation of the whole church for the task of evangelism*
For too long we have assumed that evangelism was the
province of only a few professionals, or a task that the pastor
alone could do (in addition to the multitude of other duties
the pastor faces every day).

Such a view is not faithful to the New Testament, nor is it
realistic if the challenges of the coming decades are to be
met. The task is simply too overwhelming. Professor Michael
Green has rightly said that 'whenever Christianity has been
at its most healthy, evangelism has stemmed from the local
church, and has had a noticeable impact on the surrounding area. I do not believe that the re-Christianisation of the
West can take place without the renewal of local churches
in this whole area of evangelism.' (Michael Green, *Evangelism Through the Local Church*, London: Hodder & Stoughton,
1990, p. ix).

The early Church spread not only by the preaching of
those few who were gifted as preachers and evangelists —
important as they were — but also through the quiet and
faithful witness of ordinary Christians to their pagan neighbours. Paul wrote to the young Thessalonian church, 'The
Lord's message rang out from you not only in Macedonia
and Achaia — your faith in God has become known everywhere' (1 Thessalonians 1: 8). He likewise commended the
Christians in Rome 'because your faith is being reported all
over the world' (Romans 1: 8). When persecution broke out
against the Church in Jerusalem, Luke tells us, 'all except
the apostles were scattered . . . . Those who had been scattered
preached the word wherever they went' (Acts 8: 1, 4).

That pattern of total mobilisation for evangelism —
including both the clergy and the laity — must be repeated
today if the Church is to spread the Gospel effectively.
Professor George Hunter has written, 'Western Christianity

needs a multitude of intentional missionary congregations — churches that will abandon the Christendom model of ministry as merely nurturing the faithful — whose primary mission will be to reach and disciple people who do not yet believe.' (George G. Hunter III, 'Can the West be Won? Christianity Today, December 16, 1991, p. 44). The Archbishop of Canterbury, Dr George Carey, has warned, 'Enthusiasm for evangelism won't amount to much if the hearts of those already in our churches are not recharged with the apostolic urgency and zeal that marked the apostle Paul. We need a regeneration of heart, mind, and will, so that others may see Christ in his people and perceive us to be a sacrament of his presence. Then, I suspect, they will believe.' (Archbishop George Carey, 'Recovering the Apostles' Zeal' Christianity Today, December 16, 1991, p. 20).

This has, of course, broad implications for church life. It means we must focus more intently on discipleship training — training which includes evangelism. It means we repent of our compromises and our failure to demonstrate the transforming power and love of Christ in our lives, and we learn afresh what it means to be salt and light in a decaying and dark world. Often the unbelieving world rejects our message because it sees no difference between Christians and non-Christians.

It means also that we encourage the discovery and development of the spiritual gift of evangelism in all of its manifestations. Within the church God 'gave some to be apostles, some to be prophets, some to be evangelists, and some to be pastors and teachers' (Ephesians 4: 11). That gift has never been withdrawn from the Church. Some will exercise that gift with children or youth; some will exercise it with their neighbours or business associates; still others will exercise it in a public preaching ministry. But however it is exercised, the special gift of evangelism should be an inherent part of the Church's total ministry, not an isolated or independent work divorced from the Church or even opposed by it.

### 3. A willingness to explore new methods and new fields

It is no coincidence that those churches which are most effective in reaching their neighbourhoods and cities for Christ are often those which are the most flexible and adaptable in their methods. For example, just because we think unchurched people *ought* to come to Sunday morning worship does not mean that they *will* come. It may have been true in a previous generation, but not today in many countries. And if that is a church's only channel for contact with those who are not its members, it should not be surprised to see its roles dwindle and few people come to faith in Christ.

To reach a neighbourhood or a community for Christ will require creative, careful, and prayerful strategic thinking. Methods which have worked in the past to make people aware of the Church and draw them into its programmes will not necessarily work in a media-saturated age. The competition for attention is too great. It has been estimated that 'the average American is exposed to 1800 commercial messages each day . . . . less than 2% of those messages actually slice through the clutter to penetrate the person's consciousness.' (Ministry Currents, January-March, 1992, p. 5).

Churches will need to learn from each other, and to plan together as they develop new strategies and methods of outreach. They will need to address honestly the barriers that keep people from Christ and their particular church, and then think of every way possible to overcome those barriers. In America some churches are starting Saturday evening services (in addition to those on Sunday) because they have found unbelievers in their areas are more open to attending then. This, of course, is not necessarily the right pattern for other churches; the main point is that we need to stand back and be creative. The old quip is still true, that the deadliest words in the church are 'but this is the way we have always done it'. Paul declared, 'Though I am free and belong to no man, I make myself a slave to everyone, to win as many as possible. .... I have become all things to all men so that by all possible means I might save some. I do all this for the sake of the gospel' (1 Corinthians 9:19, 22-23).

In many communities that will mean developing specific programmes to meet the needs of specialized groups — mothers, singles, single parents, teenagers, the elderly, business people, etc. Each of those groups has particular felt needs, and these often can form the point of contact between them and the church.

I do not want to be misunderstood, however. Evangelism is more than methods, and in fact methods can get in the way of authentic evangelism. Methods are necessary, but methods also can easily become ends in themselves instead of tools or means of evangelism.

A careful study of the New Testament will show that the earliest Christians used every possible legitimate method to reach others with the message of Christ — door to door evangelism, open air preaching, personal contact with relatives and friends, literature, etc. However, the method was never allowed to obscure the message. Church growth expert Charles Kelly has rightly commented, 'We can't be so caught up in trying to reach the contemporary world that we lose sight of God's agenda for the church. And that is a temptation.' (Baptist Press Service, March 17, 1992).

### 4. A total and unconditional dependence on God to accomplish His purposes

In recalling his ministry in the rough-and-tumble Greek seaport of Corinth — on the surface a singularly unpromising field for evangelism — Paul confessed, 'My message and my preaching were not with wise and persuasive words' (1 Corinthians 2: 4). He then stated the secret of his success there: 'I planted the seed, Apollos watered it, but God made it grow' (1 Corinthians 3: 6).

To me there has always been a wondrous mystery to the preaching of the Gospel. We are commanded to be faithful in proclaiming the Word — and yet at the same time every success, every advance, no matter how slight, is possible only because God has been at work by the Holy Spirit. He is the one who gives us the message; He is the one who leads us to those He has prepared; He is the one who brings conviction of sin and new life. There is power in the Word of God.

When we understand that truth, it frees us from the temptation to use manipulation or pressure. It also should free us from pride and boasting, because we know that God alone must receive the credit for whatever is accomplished.

When we understand that truth, we also will realise the urgency of prayer in evangelism. My own ministry, I am convinced, has only been possible because of the countless men and women who have prayed. I never stand before an audience without sensing those prayers, and sensing also my own dependence on God the Holy Spirit to accomplish His work. Dr John Stott has said, 'Without the work of the Spirit, whether in his general operation or in his special ministries, the Church's work and witness are bound to be ineffective.... Before Christ sent the Church into the world, he sent the Spirit to the Church. The same order must be observed today.' (John R. W. Stott, 'The Great Commission' *One Race, One Gospel, One Task: Official Papers of the World Congress on Evangelism, Berlin, 1966* Minneapolis: World Wide Publications, Vol. 1, pp. 55-56). The words from Zechariah should be written indelibly on our hearts and minds: '"Not by might nor by power, but by my Spirit," says the Lord Almighty' (Zechariah 4: 6).

As we stand on the threshold of a new century — and a new millennium — what is God saying to us?

If we are among those who have been indifferent to God, His message is clear: Come to me while there is still time. I made you; I love you; I have provided the way for you to come to know me personally by faith in Christ. By faith open your heart and life to me. I alone can bring you lasting peace and hope and new life. Don't delay coming to me any longer. 'For God so loved the world that he gave his one and only Son, that whoever believes in him shall not perish but have eternal life. For God did not send his Son into the world to condemn the world, but to save the world through him' (John 3: 16-17).

To His people, however, God is saying another message today. He is telling us to be faithful to Christ, and to be faithful to His calling to point others to Him by our words and by our deeds. Will the 21st Century mark the greatest advance the Christian Church has ever known — or the greatest defeat? Now is the time to begin to answer that question, by renewing our commitment to Christ and rising to the challenge of evangelism in our world.

At his enthronement in April 1991, as the 103rd Archbishop of Canterbury, Dr Carey took as his text the compelling words of the apostle Paul: 'For necessity is laid upon me; yea, woe is unto me, if I preach not the gospel!' (1 Corinthians 9: 16, KJV). Archbishop Carey's words bear repeating: 'It will be woe to us if we preach religion instead of the gospel; woe to us if we seek to live off the inheritance of the past and fail to build on those foundations for the future; woe to us if we preach a message that looks only towards inner piety and does not relate our faith to the world around. . . . And woe to us if we fail to hand on to future generations the unsearchable riches of Christ which are the very heartbeat of the Church and its mission.' (Quoted in *The Daily Telegraph*, April 20, 1991).

That is our challenge as we stand at the threshold of the third millennium.

All biblical quotations are from the
New International Version
unless otherwise noted

# 2

## THE BIBLE IN THE TWENTY-FIRST CENTURY
### Confronting the Next Frontier

DAVID G. BURKE

PETER J. WOSH

LAURA GOOSTREE

*Introduction: Tradition and Innovation in American Culture*

A creative tension between the forces of tradition and the forces of innovation has been a driving force in the development of American culture. The desire to innovate allowed newcomers to the continent to discard certain aspects of their heritage in order to settle a new country, develop a democracy, and invent America. At the same time, traditional mores and social structures stabilized these innovative trends and allowed for the forward movement of the development of the nation. Of course, this process contains its conflicts and ambiguities. Certain aspects of traditionalism have always appealed to the narrowly backward-looking, who resist change simply because it is change. On the other hand, innovation has led in some instances to lawlessness and exploitation, in part because there may be no social point of reference to mandate appropriate public and private responses to change.

The American imagination has been shaped by dichotomous images which mediate the tension between tradition and innovation. Two of those significant images have been those of savagery and of civilisation. Much of the development of American culture and custom has been the desire to promote the blessings of civilisation in order to subdue the savage trends of the frontier. This was true whether the frontier was the Pennsylvania woodlands or the

Great Plains. In many cases, civilisation as promoted in this process consisted of a volatile amalgam of tradition and innovation. Thus the forces of change and of stability united in the face of a common cultural goal — facing the unknown.[1]

Any discussion of the future of the Bible in American culture needs to be rooted in an understanding of the ways in which the Bible has played an important role as an instrument both of change and of stability in the various frontiers of the American experience. While there exists an obvious physical frontier defined by American geography, other, more intangible new frontiers have also been explored and developed to contribute to American national development. These new frontiers include, but are not limited to social, technological, industrial and cultural frontiers. They encompass modes of communication and rates of literacy. They are concerned with the urban experience as well as the rural, and have been shaped by the forces of industrialisation and immigration. Above all, these frontiers have been what Walt Whitman referred to as 'democratic vistas,' the places and cultural elements which will continue to shape our national experience into the next century and beyond.

### The American Bible Society in the Nineteenth Century

In 1814, the Massachusettes Missionary Society employed two Presbyterians, Samuel J. Mills and Daniel Smith, to tour what was at that time the southern and western United States and gather information concerning the religious state of Americans living in these isolated territories. Mills and Smith submitted a series of reports which shocked the

[1]Henry Nash Smith, *Virgin Land: The American West as Symbol and Myth* (Cambridge and London: Harvard University Press, 1950); John G. Cawelti, *Adventure, Mystery and Romance: Formula Stories as Art and Popular Culture* (Chicago and London: The University of Chicago Press, 1976), pp. 192-259.

sensibilities of evangelical Christians. At Natchez, Mississippi, the travelling missionaries found people 'ashamed to buy a Bible. When they ask for one at a bookstore they often think it necessary to frame some frivolous apology for their conduct.' Western Florida included 'some American families . . . *who never saw a Bible, nor heard of Jesus Christ*'. In Tennessee, these pious Presbyterians observed the typical 'vices, common in our western country... intemperance — profanity — Sabbath breaking — gambling, etc.' High waters prevented Mills and Smith from thoroughly exploring the river towns along the Ohio River, but they noted that one county seat in the Illinois Territory 'is continually deluged like most other towns in the Territories, by a far worse flood of impiety and iniquity.' Summarising their findings, the missionaries sadly lamented the 'dreadful famine of the *written*, as well as the *preached* word of God, which prevails in this country.'[2]

As they completed their tour in 1815, Samuel Mills and Daniel Smith could not have predicted that the United States was on the verge of an extraordinary revolution in technology, transportation and communication which would end this famine of Scripture and place the written word in the hands of most Americans. The American Bible Society constituted an integral component of that revolution. Driven by a combination of early nineteenth-century entrepreneurial spirit and evangelical zeal, the Society's work possessed extraordinary implications both for the greater circulation of the Sacred Scriptures and for American religion in general.

New York City's role as the economic centre of the young republic is well-documented. What is perhaps less well-known is that nineteenth-century New York also served as the religious capital of evangelical America. The same

[2]Samuel J. Mills and Daniel Smith, *Report of A Missionary Tour Through That Part of the United States Which Lies West of the Allegany Mountains; Performed Under the Direction of the Massachusetts Missionary Society* (Andover: Flagg and Gould, 1815), pp. 27, 29, 24, 17, 20.

economic forces which created South Street and Wall Street simultaneously stimulated the founding and growth of multidenominational nonprofit religious philanthropies like the American Bible Society (1816) and American Tract Society (1825). These national, urban-based institutions shared Mills' and Smith's commitments to evangelizing the United States and bringing God's message to all Americans. They fuelled and reinforced the outpouring of religious sentiment commonly defined as the 'Second Great Awakening.' The Bible Society proved especially innovative in applying the most modern technological, organisational, and administrative techniques available in the nineteenth century to the cause of Scripture publication and distribution.[3]

[3]Standard histories of Bible and Tract Societies include: Clifford S. Griffin, *Their Brothers' Keepers: Moral Stewardship in the United States, 1800-1865* (New Brunswick: Rutgers University Press, 1960); and Charles I. Foster, *An Errand of Mercy: The Evangelical United Front, 1790-1837* (Chapel Hill: University of North Carolina Press, 1960). Paul Boyer links these institutions with American urbanisation in *Urban Masses and Moral Order in America* (Cambridge: Harvard University Press, 1978). More recent treatments of organisations connected with the nineteenth century 'benevolent empire', stressing different themes can be found in Anne M. Boylan, *Sunday School: The Formation of an American Institution, 1790-1880* (New Haven: Yale University Press, 1988); Gregory Singleton, 'Protestant Voluntary Organisations and the Shaping of Victorian America,' in Daniel Walker Howe, ed., *Victorian America* (Philadelphia: University of Pennsylvania Press, 1976), pp. 47-58; David Paul Nord, 'The Evangelical Origins of Mass Media in America, 1815-1835,' *Journalism Monographs*, Number 88, (Columbia: Association for Education in Journalism and Mass Communication, May 1984); Peter J. Wosh, 'Bibles, Benevolence and Emerging Bureaucracy: The Persistence of the American Bible Society, 1816-1890.' Ph. D. dissertation, New York University, 1988; and John B. Jentz, 'Artisans, Evangelicals and the City: A Social History of Abolition and Labor Reform in Early New York, Ph.D. dissertation, City University of New York, 1977. For an important and interesting work on the British & Foreign Bible Society, consult Leslie Howsam, *Cheap Bibles: Nineteenth-Century Publishing and the British and Foreign Bible Society* (New York: Cambridge University Press, 1991).

*Innovation in the Bible Movement*

Technological innovation constituted a cornerstone of the nineteenth-century Bible movement. Shortly after the establishment of the American Bible Society, the Board of Managers directed 'their first exertions . . . towards the procurement of well executed stereotype plates.' Stereotyping, which revolutionised the printing trades and fostered the mass publication of standardised works such as tracts and Bibles, remained a key element in the transformation of the nation's print industry. Other innovations, including steam presses and Fourdrinier papermaking machines, were also adapted quickly by the Bible societies, thus allowing the production and circulation of modestly-priced Bibles on an unprecedented scale.[4]

Religious publishing dominated New York City's burgeoning book and periodical market throughout the nineteenth century. Large mechanised printing plants, employing hundreds of workers and utilising steam presses, had transformed the metropolis into nation's information capital by mid-century. The great book publishers were concentrated in Manhattan, and by 1856 New York produced 38 per cent of the sixteen million dollars worth of books manufactured in the United States. Still, the leading historian of American book publishing has observed that 'no trade publisher could even approach' the volume of receipts amassed by the American Bible Society in 1855, and the evangelical publishing houses remained among the industry's principal innovators. In the judgment of one

---

[4]American Bible Society, *First Annual Report,* (New York: J. Seymour, 1817), p. 10; Nord, 'The Evangelical Origins of Mass Media,' discusses these innovations in detail, as does Thomas Boomershine, 'Response to Richard M. Harley, "New Media for Communicating the Bible: the Potential and the Problems,"' in Howard Clark Kee, ed., *The Bible for the Twenty-first Century: Papers for the American Bible Society's 175th Anniversary Symposium on the Bible* (New York: American Bible Society and Trinity Press Int., forthcoming, 1992), pp. 181-186.

recent historian of American journalism, the Bible and
Tract societies 'helped lay the foundation for mass media in
America through their pioneering work in mass printing
and mass distribution of the printed word.'[5]

Immigration, industrialisation, westward expansion, and
the growing internationalisation of American missionary
work all stimulated the American Bible Society to remain
on the cutting edge of technological advancement throughout the nineteenth century. Irish and German immigrants
composed significant elements in north-eastern cities and
mid-western farming villages by the 1840s, large concen-
trations of Chinese workers laboured in California and
western mining towns by the 1870s, and unprecedented
numbers of arrivals from southern and eastern Europe
transformed the entire character of the American population by the turn of the century. By 1920, over fifty per cent
of all Americans lived in cities, and industrialisation completely altered the character of daily life. The linguistic and
educational diversity of this increasingly urban and foreign-
born population placed new demands on Bible Societies.
Scripture distribution agencies needed to remain aware of
rapidly changing population trends and immigration patterns. They struggled to produce and provide a diverse
range of Bibles in an extraordinary array of languages and
dialects. In 1900 alone, for example, the Massachusetts
Bible Society distributed Scriptures in the following languages: Danish, Swedish, Norwegian, Finnish, Italian,
French, Portuguese, Spanish, Latin, Greek, Hebrew, Welsh,
Dutch, German, Armenian, Arabic, Bulgarian, Gaelic, Bo-
hemian, Russian, Polish, Lettish, Chinese, Hungarian, Syriac,
Lithuanian, and Malay.[6]

---

[5]John K. Tebbel, *A History of Book Publishing in the United States* (New
York: R. R. Bowker, 1972), Volume I, pp. 229, 279, 588; Nord, 'Evangelical Origins of Mass Media', p. 2. See Edward K. Spann, *The New Metropolis*,
pp. 206-410; Sean Wilentz, *Chants Democratic*, pp. 129-132; Alan Pred,
*Urban Growth and the Circulation of Cities*, p. 28.

[6]American Bible Society, *Annual Report* (1900), p. 50.

Organisational innovation complemented and reinforced the Bible movement's technological sophistication. The American Bible Society emerged as one of the nation's most highly centralised, capitalised and systematised operations by the middle of the nineteenth century. During its early years, the American Bible Society created its own printing department (1845), established a bindery (1848), made its own stereotype plates (1851), manufactured its own electrotyping equipment (1853), and brought all of its operations under one roof in the magnificent five-story Bible House on Astor Place in New York City (1853). The Society employed dozens of travelling Bible Agents nationwide, each of whom co-ordinated Scripture distribution in specific territories throughout the United States and abroad. Hundreds of local voluntary auxiliary societies affiliated with the national institution. They systematically organised Bible distribution by county, city, and ward in order to provide adequate numbers of Scriptures for every American community.

As a transportation network of canals and railroads gradually knit the United States into an integrated political and economic unit, and as communication advances like the telegraph increased the speed of communication, the American Bible Society marshalled these modern technological miracles in the service of circulating God's Word. Bible Agents, colporteurs, and travelling missionaries remained at the edge of the American frontier, bringing the Book to newly established communities and to settlements in the nation's most remote regions. As early as 1849, the Society stationed an Agent in California. The Rev. Frederic Buel, who accepted this assignment, remarked on 'the strange mingling of faces, complexions, garbs and dresses' in his new field, observing that the missionary possibilities in this relatively inaccessible corner of the continent exceeded most areas of the globe. Emerging Christian populations created unprecedented opportunities for carrying the Bible to new audiences. Efforts to reach the 'missionary frontier' necessitated sophisticated institutional programmes and approaches.[7]

*Democratising Influences in the Bible Movement*

The Bible Societies' technological and organisational innovations fundamentally altered the ways in which nineteenth-century Americans viewed the Bible. Three aspects of this transformation appear especially relevant for our understanding of future trends in Bible work. First, popular mass accessibility to the printed Bible fostered an unprecedented array of new English language translations. Only one new American revision of the *King James Version* (KJV) had appeared between 1650 and 1820. By contrast, American translators and scholars constructed fourteen major new English language works in the forty years following 1820. Some grounded their writings in divine revelation, while others carefully consulted ancient texts not available to the King James translators in 1611. Cumulatively, whether based on revelation, scholarship, or sectarian interest, these new Bibles challenged the concept of an 'authorised version' and hinted that different Americans might benefit from different versions of the Holy Scriptures.[8]

Noah Webster (1758-1843), the noted lexicographer and an orthodox New England Congregationalist, published his own version of the Bible in 1833. Observing that 'the language of the Bible has no inconsiderable influence in forming and preserving our own national language,' he considered his revision 'not merely a matter of expedience,

[7]Frederick Buel, quoted in Creighton Lacy, *The Word Carrying Giant: The Growth of the American Bible Society* (Pasadena: William Carey Library, 1977), p. 101. Margaret T. Hills, 'Production and Supply of Scriptures, 1831-1860,' ABS unpublished Historical Essay # 18, Part III, pp. 8-36.

[8]Harold P. Scanlin, 'Bible Translation by American Individuals,' in Ernst Frerichs, ed., *The Bible and Bibles in America* (Atlanta: Scholars Press, 1987). See also Margaret T. Hills, ed., *The English Bible in America* (New York: American Bible Society and New York Public Library, 1962).

but of moral duty.' Webster realised that the traditional *King James Version* contained serious limitations that decreased its utility for the average nineteenth-century reader. 'A version of the Scriptures for popular use,' he declared, 'should consist of words expressing the sense which is most common, in popular usage.' Accordingly, Webster modified obscure passages, standardised the grammar, and eliminated 'some quaint and vulgar phrases' in an effort to make the document more accessible. Shaping the Word of God for a newly-developing mass readership emerged as a new challenge and an urgent necessity.[9]

A second outgrowth of the Bible movement resulted from the increased accessibility of the Bible to ordinary people. Evangelicals like Alexander Campbell and Barton Stone established popular movements based on 'no creed but the Bible.' Everyman and everywoman now seemed competent to examine the Scriptures with a fresh eye and to discern his or her own eternal truths. Ironically, the creation of institutions such as the American Bible Society unintentionally raised new questions concerning authority in the young Republic and reinforced the democratising influences evident in many aspects of nineteenth-century American religion.[10]

[9]Noah Webster, *The Holy Bible, containing the Old and New Testaments, in the Common Version, with Amendments of the Language* (New Haven: Durrie & Peck, 1833), pp. iii, iv, v.

[10]Nathan O. Hatch, 'Sola Scriptura and Novus Ordo Seclorum,' in Nathan O. Hatch and Mark Noll, *The Bible in America: Essays in Cultural History* (New York: Oxford University Press, 1982), pp. 73-74. On the Federalist Standing Order and the role of these new institutions, see Peter Dobkin Hall, *The Organization of American Culture, 1700-1900; Private Institutions, Elites, and the Origins of American Nationality* (New York: New York University Press, 1982). For a fresh new interpretation of popular religion in nineteenth century America, consult Nathan O. Hatch, *The Democratisation of American Christianity* (New Haven: Yale University Press, 1989).

The Bible became an important battleground through-out the nineteenth century for reformers, political activists, and defenders of the status quo, all of whom quoted Scripture to reinforce particular positions and viewpoints. Slaveholders argued that biblical references to the 'curse of Ham' and similar passages justified the existence of the 'peculiar institution', while abolitionists used other biblical injunctions to undermine these arguments. Traditionalists pointed to biblical authority as a legitimate reason for justifying women's subordinate roles in the church, yet feminists and suffragists promoted new interpretations of Scripture to advocate greater use of women's gifts. Americans could not even agree on the Bible's prescriptions for peace and non-violence, as advocates of just war theories clashed with biblical peace activists. Greater proliferation of the Word and the democratisation of religion revealed the extent to which Americans differed over interpretation and doctrine.[11]

Finally, the Bible movement encouraged Christians to think of the Sacred Scriptures primarily as a written document. The essential orality of the Gospel message was somewhat diminished in the new world of mass print. Disputes over precise wording, disagreements over any departure from established texts, and the growth of biblical criticism within the scholarly world testified to the new concern with precise written meanings.

If the growth of Bible Societies promoted some democratising tendencies in American religion, countervailing pressures also resulted. 'Cheap Bibles' encouraged Americans to process religious information in new ways and created new orthodoxies based on fidelity to the *written*, as opposed to the *preached*, word. Bible Societies satisfied the needs of

---

[11]The series of articles in Ernest R. Sandeen, *The Bible and Social Reform* (Philadelphia: Fortress Press, 1982) addresses these differing interpretations and divisions.

American missionaries in producing Scriptures for the
south and west and introduced new audiences to the Gospel
message. The multiplicity of versions, religious movements,
denominations, and interpretations, however, meant that
the message of the preached word remained diverse and
subject to the forces fragmenting American Christianity.

Twentieth century Bible work built on these developments, but the Bible Societies also operated within a dramatically altered political, social, and technological environment. The growing internationalisation of the Bible
movement opened new missionary frontiers and increased
pressures for new translation strategies. The establishment
of the United Bible Societies in 1946 created the possibility
of a co-ordinated, systematic approach to Bible translation
in third world countries with low rates of literacy. Further,
new vehicles for communicating and distributing Scripture
emerged as technology changed. Initially, the Bible Societies applied new technologies primarily to distribution
and marketing activities: Bible vans and airplanes opened
previously inaccessible areas to the Word, direct mail
emerged as an innovative fundraising strategy, sound re-
cordings brought the Gospel message to the visually im-
paired, and educational films cast the story of the Bible in
new formats. By the mid-twentieth century, however, the
most exciting developments appeared to be occurring in
the area of translation itself.[12]

### Tradition and Innovation in Bible Translation

Until the middle of the twentieth century most Bible translation work was done according to a methodology that
could be called 'literal' or 'formal equivalence' translation.
This approach, epitomised in English by the *King James*

---

[12]Creighton Lacy, *The Word Carrying Giant*, pp. 153-173; Boyd Daniels,
ed., 'The UBS At 40,' *United Bible Societies Bulletin*, Second/Third Quar-
ters, 1986.

*Version,* aims to represent the style and structure of the original language texts as directly as possible in the receptor language. The model for translating is thus one of formal or direct correspondence in which both the words and the grammatical patterns of the ancient biblical texts have their formal correspondences in the receptor language translation.

With its common emphasis on word for word equivalence, this model would appear to promise precision. More often than not, however, it yields a translation in very unnatural English which obscures meaning for the reader/hearer. Familiar examples would include such literalisms, 'holy of holies', or 'Song of Songs', which are used in English to represent the Hebrew form for indicating superlative degree. And that same sort of literalism can apply to syntax. Consider, for example, the tortuous English of the *King James Version* at Nehemiah 13.26: 'nevertheless even him did outlandish women cause to sin'. The fourth century dictum of Jerome, *et verborum ordo mysterium est,* came generally to be understood to mean that even the word order has sacred character. That one belief has tended to dominate Bible translation until this century.[13]

By the 1960s, this literal approach to translation was beginning to be superseded by the method of 'functional equivalence', in which translation is done in terms of larger thought units — whole sentences or even paragraphs rather than single words — involving 'meaning for meaning' equivalence. Emphasis in this approach is placed on achieving the clearest communication of the meaning of the Bible's original language texts in the modern receptor language. Functional equivalence has become the dominant model in translation since being pioneered in the 1960s by the American Bible Society's Eugene A. Nida and

---

[13]Harvey Minkoff, 'How Bible Translations Differ,' *Biblical Archaeology Review* (March-April, 1992), p. 66.

his colleagues in the United Bible Societies. The first two complete Bibles produced with this method of translation were the *Versión Popular* in Spanish and the *Today's English Version* (TEV) or *Good News Bible* in English. Both translations arc still widely used today.[14]

When the *TEV* first appeared it received condemnation in some conservative circles. It was often mistaken for a paraphrase because its English form made it appear so freshly different from the traditional feel of word-for-word translations. That was because the sentence elements of the original language syntax were so regularly and freshly reconfigured in English in order to provide the clearest English structure for the reader. It is important to understand that a paraphrase is a restatement of a text or phrase *within the same language,* often done by expanding words in order to clarify meaning. In contrast to paraphrase, a translation is the communication of a message *from one language to another.* Whether a Bible translation is accomplished by formal or functional equivalent methods, it is a translation because it works from the Bible's original lan-

---

[14]Alan S. Duthie, *Bible Translations and How to Choose Between Them* (Exeter: Paternoster Press, 1985), p. 34. Duthie contends that the most 'accurate' or 'faithful' translation is the one that best expresses 'the *same meaning,* first expressed in language A . . . in language B.' Further, he notes, 'Those who receive a communication translation [i.e., a functional equivalence translation] in language B have the opportunity of responding to the translated message in language A. If any type of translation is appropriate for the Bible, this surely is it!' For further background on the theoretics and principles of functional equivalence, see also Jan de Waard and Eugene A. Nida, *From One Language to Another* (Nashville: Thomas Nelson, 1986), pp. 36-44. In their words, 'The translation process [of functional equivalence] has been defined on the basis that receptors of a translation should comprehend the translated text to such an extent that they can understand how the original receptors must have understood the original text,' p. 36. See also Eugene A. Nida, *Toward a Science of Translating* (Leiden: E. J. Brill, 1964), pp. 171-175.

guage texts in Greek, Hebrew and Aramaic into a modern receptor language.[15]

In a review and assessment of recent English Bible translations, Donald A. Carson has acknowledged that there is now 'widespread recognition of the primacy of [functional equivalence] as the best controlling model in Bible translation.'[16] Used in dozens of current UBS projects around the globe, the methodology and principles of functional equivalence now dominate Bible translation practice everywhere. Among English translations completed since the pioneering TEV, there are very few that have not been influenced by the principles of this translation model. The turnaround to broad acceptance has been remarkable and has taken place within a rather short period of time:

> Today most competent translators recognise that 'literal translation' and 'free translation' exist on the same spectrum, differentiable in the extremes but nevertheless unavoidably connected; that meaning and form, though intertwined, are not only differentiable, but that very frequently meaning in the donor language has to be packaged in a quite different form in the receptor language; that translation is never a mechanical exercise, but entails countless decisions as to the text's meaning; that meaning is not only referential but may embrace subtle overtones, emotional loading, degrees of naturalness, pragmatic associations, implicit moral obligation, and much more.[17]

With the New Testament published in 1991, the American Bible Society's *Contemporary English Version* (CEV) incorporates significant new information on discourse structure and exemplifies the functional equivalent model in its most

---

[15]See further, Duthie, *Bible Translations*, p. 33, and the literature.

[16]Donald A. Carson, 'New Bible Translations: An Assessment and Prospect,' in Howard Clark Kee, ed., *The Bible for the Twenty-first Century: Papers from the American Bible Society's 175th Anniversary Symposium on the Bible* (New York: ABS and Trinity Press Int., forthcoming, 1992), p. 36.

[17]*Ibid.*, p. 38. See further, Michael F. Kopesec, 'A Translator's Perspective on Meaning,' *Occasional Papers in Translation and Textlinguistics* 2 (1988), pp. 9-19.

contemporary refinement, as laid out in its statement of Guiding Principles:

> The translation technique to be followed will be that of 'functional equivalence', which requires an *analysis* of words and grammatical constructions and a *restructuring* in a form that is clear, natural, and unambiguous. . . . Every attempt will be made to represent accurately the *meaning* (not always the form!) of the biblical text at a level most appropriate to the audience.[18]

Even the 1990 *New Revised Standard Version* (NRSV) translators, in bringing the 1952 *Revised Standard Version* (RSV) up to date, found it necessary to be 'as literal as possible, as free as necessary.' The impact of the functional equivalence model on this revision, which stands in lineal descent from the KJV, is clearly signalled in its preface 'To the Reader,' which maintains that the biblical message 'must not be disguised in phrases that are no longer clear, or hidden under words that have changed or lost their meaning; it must be presented in language that is direct and plain and meaningful to people today.'[19]

*Trailblazing Multimedia Translation*

Another pioneering application of the principles of functional equivalence will be used to translate the Scriptures of the twenty-first century into new audiovisual and multimedia forms that go beyond the familiar bounds of print. At the close of the twentieth century we are in the midst of a groundshift in communications technology and the resulting media environment. Certain realities are already apparent — 98 per cent of American households have at least one television set. It is estimated that by 1995, 85 per cent of these homes will also have a videocassette recorder. Per-

---

[18]*'Contemporary English Version:* Guiding Principles,' American Bible Society Unpublished Internal Document, March 11, 1992, p. 2.
[19]'To the Reader,' Preface to the *New Revised Standard Version* (New York: American Bible Society, 1990), pp. iii-iv.

sonal computer ownership is on the rise, and the era of various interactive and multimedia formats linking video and computer is in its beginning stages.[20]

We are increasingly becoming a people who prefer our communication and information media to supply sound and images and not simply silent words in print. We are presently witnessing the translation of a sizeable population segment into 'post-literacy'; that is, people who can read, but who, for various reasons, increasingly choose not to. In the view of media critic Neil Postman:

> We have reached . . . critical mass in that electronic media have decisively and irreversibly changed the character of our symbolic environment. We are now a culture whose information, ideas and epistemology are given form by television, not by the printed word.[21]

While Postman views this groundshift as essentially ominous, there are biblical scholars who see instead great potential in this change — potential for communicating Scripture not only to post-literate populations, but even to pre-literate and illiterate populations around the globe. Thomas Boomershine, a scholar concerned with the oral character of Scripture and its relation to contemporary media forms, understands this shift in the human consciousness to be as dramatic and far-reaching as the earlier transition from orality to print-oriented literacy.[22]

For increasing numbers of people — especially the young — screen-centred media forms have replaced the book as the intimate medium of choice. Taking note of this phenomenon, in 1989 the American Bible Society initiated a re-

[20]Fern Lee Hagedorn, 'Why Multimedia Translations? An American Bible Society Perspective,' *United Bible Societies Bulletin* 160/161 (1991), p. 21.

[21]Neil Postman, *Amusing Ourselves to Death: Public Discourse in the Age of Show Business* (New York: Penguin, 1985), p. 28.

[22]Thomas E. Boomershine, 'Biblical Megatrends: Towards a Paradigm for the Interpretation of the Bible in Electronic Media,' in Kent Harold Richards, ed., *Society of Biblical Literature 1987 Seminar Papers* (Atlanta: Scholars Press, 1987), pp. 144-157.

search and development project, under the guidance of
Fern Lee Hagedorn, to explore the possibilities for translating Scripture in the new multimedia forms. Multimedia
translation has been defined by the American Bible Society's chief translation officer, Dr. Barclay M. Newman, as
follows:

> A multimedia translation combines a faithful functional equivalent
> rendering of the source text with supplementary audiovisual features
> that maximise the potential for both a proper understanding of and
> an appropriate response to the message of the text.[23]

Newman has further observed that '[t]he combination of
sight and sound creates a context where the viewer can
potentially become more fully involved in the message of
the text than might be possible in either a public or private
reading of a print-medium translation.'[24]

How can the Bible continue to be a primary means by
which God communicates to people, when their chief
source of information is now a television set or computer
terminal rather than a book? This is the underlying question that has driven this research project. A key finding of
the American Bible Society multimedia research project
underscores the urgency of the Society's entrance into
multimedia translation work. This finding is that there
simply are no Bible audiovisuals of any type extant today
that have been produced on the basis of a translation
approach, from an examination of the original language
Bible texts. Further, this examination of the original texts
must occur not only in terms of word meaning but also their
sound and image characteristics.[25]

Application of the principles of functional equivalence
translation to communication of the Scriptures in the new
electronic screen-centred media means that a translation in

[23]Hagedorn, p. 22.
[24]*Ibid.*
[25]Boomershine, 'Biblical Megatrends,' p. 151.

video, for example, should present sounds and images that are the functional equivalents of the original sounds and images that were evoked by the original storytelling events in the first century AD for the people in the audience. In the pilot translation in video form of Mark's story of the Gerasene Demoniac (Mark 5.1-20) which has been prepared by the American Bible Society, the actual words used in the translation have been chosen in order to convey the sounds, the original connotations of the words and something of their rhythm and volume in addition to their denotative meanings. The episodic arrangement of the words also calls attention to the units of sound in which the story was told. This serves to clarify the points of emphasis or climax as well as the major pauses within the story.

This American Bible Society video translation is one of functional equivalence because it presents sounds and images that are the functional equivalents of the original sounds and images of the story of the Gerasene Demoniac. Before this story about Jesus's healing of the Gerasene began to be transmitted in written form it was told or recited, and its original character in this initial period of oral transmission was one of a combination of sounds heard and images invited. In order to prepare a video translation, or 'transmediasation,' of such a story in electronic media forms it is necessary to present the story as sounds and screen images rather than as printed marks on a page. That requires a different process, both for the study of the original language text and for producing a translation. A whole new set of factors come into play; such things as rhythm, intonation, attitude, volume, repetition and emotion have influence on the oral/aural dimension in ways that have not usually been considered relevant to print translations. In order to move towards a functional equivalence of the resonance of the sounds and rhythms of the ancient biblical text, the music track also has to be carefully conceived. Regarding the development of images, Boomershine has stated that

> The representation of the images of the story in this treatment is highly symbolic and fluid. Symbolic images, video montage, and faces that have visual connection with the story are all visual elements of the treatment. . . . The narrative structure of this treatment creates a degree of involvement and identification with a contemporary young person who experiences the basic dynamics of the encounter with Jesus in his encounter with a man who cares for him now. But the possibility of an allegorical interpretation is broken by the quick-cutting technique and the steady fracturing of the narrative line.[26]

The aim of the American Bible Society multimedia pilot project has been to reach those young people who are less likely to read with the word of God through screen-centred media formats. The approach of the American Bible Society research group has been twofold. One approach has been to develop a prototype video translation that would utilise contemporary music and images and electronic techniques that young people would easily relate to and understand. Such a functional equivalent video translation will not seek to depict a historical recreation of the Scripture passage, but instead offer a cinematic functional equivalent of the original storytelling event, based on scholarly re-examination of the original language text of the passage in question. The effect of this is that the modern viewer is not only addressed by the story in words, music and images but

[26]Thomas E. Boomershine, 'A Multimedia Functional Equivalent Translation of the Gerasene Demoniac (Mark 5.1-20)' (American Bible Society Unpublished Study Document, September, 1991), pp. 1-2. A cogent rationale for the Church's need to begin to convey the biblical message in electronic media forms may be found in James M. Wall, 'The Pictures Inside Our Heads,' *The Christian Century* (March 18-25, 1992), p. 291. Wall observes that 'The community that formalized the Bible expressed itself in signs and symbols. Its members pointed to a story with a beginning and an end, but this narrative is not limited by time or space. It is not just a linear narrative. It is a work of art, forged by a community of believers. . . . Its power lies not in the sequence of events it describes but in its power to transform our vision . . . The Bible is crammed with images that assault the senses . . . [and with stories] not bound by their linear shape.

also is invited to respond to it emotionally in the same way that the original storytelling event evoked an emotional response in the first-century audience member.

That the American Bible Society prototype video translation of Mark 5.1-20 has been on target in this regard is suggested by the focus group testing that has been carried out with teenagers and college students. The focus group results show clearly that, regardless of the degree to which the viewers 'liked' the film version of this story of Jesus' healing of the demon-possessed man of Gerasa, they were clearly unanimous in their reaction that they heard the underlying message clearly and forcefully — namely, that there is power and hope in Jesus for young people who may find themselves possessed by something evil that they cannot seem to control under their own power.

The second focus of the American Bible Society approach has been on the development of a supplementary study help to accompany the video translation — a learning resource that takes the form of an interactive computer programme in which the capabilities of film, still images, text, music, spoken word, graphics, and even games are combined to help young people explore the Bible story in great depth in order to learn more broadly and profoundly its relevance and meaning for their lives.

The American Bible Society research and development work into multimedia translations is still in its infancy. Much, of course, remains to be done and explored, but what has been produced in the form of prototypes shows great promise for the future. Based on a sampling of trends and developments already underway, the prospect of the twenty-first century promises to be exciting and innovative for Bible translation. As we move into the next century, the Bible Society will continue to base its translation work on a thorough examination of the source texts — whether the medium be print or non-print — as it continues to explore fresh and faithful ways of making the Scriptures accessible to those various audiences and constituencies in need of the Word of God.

*Postliteracy: The New Spiritual Frontier*

As we have seen, the tension between historical forces of tradition and innovation have played enormously significant roles in the shaping of American culture. Among other historical circumstances, technological and organisational innovations have led to the development of the modern Bible movement in America, which allowed for an unprecedented access to the Scriptures and a subsequent democratising of interpretations and uses to which Americans put the Bible. Fuelled by the need to provide people with the Scriptures in forms that they can easily understand, innovations in the practice of translation have led the American Bible Society away from traditional methods of formal equivalence into the newer methods of functional equivalence. One translation project guided by the principles of functional equivalence which will have an enormous impact on Bible work in the next century is the pioneering step into multimedia Scripture translation.

Without question, creative ways will have to be used to bring the Word to a sizeable proportion of the American population in the next century. According to figures from Reading Is Fundamental, the group that operates the largest literacy programme in the United States, up to twenty-one million Americans may be illiterate.

> Statistics collected by the organisation show that fewer than 25 per cent of high school seniors read for pleasure; 90 per cent of grade school children find television more appealing than reading, and 82 per cent of these pupils prefer video games to reading.[27]

The willingness to engage with the complexities of the printed word is not necessarily correlated to family income, and presumably education. A poll conducted by Associated Press early in 1992 indicated that 30 per cent of families that

[27]'Romancing the Book . . . Once Again,' *The New York Times*, June 21, 1992, Section 2, p. 16.

earn more than $40,000 annually report that they have no books at all in their homes.[28]

Inevitably, the creativity needed to address a post-literate relationship to books may threaten or confuse individuals who view the Scriptures primarily as the 'printed' word. Bible workers in the next century have a twofold responsibility. First, they must continue performing their traditional role: to bring the Word of God to people *where they are.* This can no longer be defined as a condition of geography as much as it is a condition of communications. Second, they must be sure to include those with traditional approaches to the Scriptures in this work. The challenge will be to mine the positive, stabilising elements of traditionalism without losing the power and will to innovate.

One way to learn how to begin this enormous task is to look to the past and to learn from what has gone before. During the nineteenth century, the spread of the Bible throughout the United States was part and parcel of the tension between tradition and innovation which created the nation. To the extent that we can learn how to balance tradition and innovation from the past and also to accept the challenge to take risks in the future in order to spread the Word of God, we will be prepared to venture into the greatest American wilderness of all — the spiritual frontier.

The task is not one of 'making' the Bible relevant. The Bible is relevant already; the problem that we face is helping a wide variety of people truly to understand that. In a way, the problem is one of feeding a multitude in the wilderness. In this case, part of our task is to help today's multitudes recognise the fact that they are in a wilderness in the first place. This is the meaning of the spiritual frontier. Somehow we need to demonstrate that the Bible is relevant because it meets needs which cannot be filled in any other way — not by buying more, or working more, or eating more, or drinking more or any of the other 'mores' used by

[28]*Ibid.*

so many in our culture to mask the knowledge of personal spiritual emptiness.

To take the Bible to someone, wherever he or she is, is increasingly to take it into a spiritual void, into an abyss of ignorance and despair. To do this effectively in the next century will mean balancing the forces of tradition with those of innovation. It will demand that all of us involved in the task be willing to take great risks, become willing to change, and be open to learning in the process. The spiritual frontier is perhaps the most daunting one of all, but the work can be done, particularly as we are empowered by the Lord to do it, for the rest of this century and beyond.

# 3

## CHRISTIAN THEOLOGY AND SCIENTIFIC CULTURE
### The Way Ahead

### THOMAS F. TORRANCE

In recent years two converging movements of thought have been transforming the intellectual interchange between theological science and natural science. Theologians have come to realise that since God makes himself known to us within the structures of space and time, there is a deeper and more significant overlap between theological and scientific concepts than they used to hold; and scientists have come to realise that the very basis of modern scientific inquiry into the nature of the universe and its inherent order has been more profoundly influenced by primary Christian ideas than they had believed. The effect of this has been to make theologians and scientists more open to each other and more ready to engage in serious dialogue with each other, not least when their points of view appear to conflict. And now a considerable body of literature has been published in which the process and results of this intellectual exchange have been registered, and institutions have been set up in order to carry forward developments in the cross-fertilising and unifying of theological and scientific culture. All this means that significant steps are being taken toward a fuller understanding of the unitary rational order of the universe in which we live.

Far from meaning that the radical differences and apparent contradictions between theological inquiry and scientific inquiry are being planned away, it means that the overlapping of these inquiries with each other, and indeed the joint meaning of their contrary features, paint for us a realistic picture of the universe as the God-given home for mankind. I am reminded here of what Michael Polanyi once wrote in explaining the kind of fusion found in the way gestalt formation takes place when forming a painting. 'This union is not a fusion of complementary parts to a whole, but a fusion of contradictory features. The flatness of the canvas is combined with a perspectival depth, which is the very opposite of flatness.'[1] It is in the formation of a perspective characterised by such a dimension of depth that we may glimpse something of the way Christian theology and scientific culture may take in the next 20 years or so.

What makes all this possible are two fundamental factors injected into scientific culture by the great Greek theologians of the early centuries as they reflected on the implications of the incarnation in Jesus Christ of the Word of God by whom all things are made, and of the concept of creation out of nothing applied to the whole cosmos of visible and invisible realities.

On the one hand, this Christian outlook destroyed the radical dualism between intelligible and material reality, or between form and matter, that had dominated the outlook of oriental and hellenic thought and had been given masterful scientific expression in Ptolemaic cosmology with its dualism between terrestrial and celestial realms. That dualism had the effect of denigrating the material and empirical realm, of denying the integrity and rationality of nature, and thus of excluding it from empirical scientific investigation. However, the Christian doctrine of the incarnation, that God and man are inseparably united in Jesus Christ within space and time, carried with it a conception of the goodness of the created order, and very different view of material reality, which together with the doctrine of the creation of all things, visible and invisible alike, out of

---

[1] Michael Polanyi, 'What is a Painting?' *The American Scholar*, vol. 39, no. 4, 1970, p. 662. Something similar is found in the formation of stereoscopic images, see *Knowing and Being*, 1969, pp. 167ff., 211ff.

nothing, gave rise to an undivided, unitary view of form and matter, in which both the intelligible and material realms are regarded as constituting together one universal rational order contingent upon God and unceasingly sustained by him. That is the fundamental conception that ultimately lies behind the modern scientific passion for unified field theory which is being pursued through penetrating deep into the unitary basis to which all immanent relations and structures permeating the whole universe point. This brings about a profound integration of ontology and epistemology, and recovers a unifying order in the very foundations of knowledge which overcomes the deep splits in human culture, and not least those between the *how* and the *why* and the *is* and the *ought,* introduced into European culture through the rationalism of the Enlightenment.

On the other hand, the Christian doctrine that Jesus Christ is the incarnate Word or Rationality of God, together with its radicalisation of the concept of creation out of nothing inherited from Judaism, meant that the rational forms immanent in the universe are not eternal and divine as hellenic philosophy and science held, but are like the rest of the created universe freely brought into being by God. A clear distinction is thus drawn been the uncreated rationality of God and the created rationality of the universe. This means that the created order of things is not necessary or timeless, for it did not have to be what it is but could have been quite different. And having been brought into existence it has been given distinctive reality, authentic rationality, integrity and reliability of its own which must be respected, utterly different as it is from God's transcendent Reality and entirely dependent or contingent on him. By contingent is meant that the universe freely created by God out of nothing contains no reason in itself why it should be what it is and why it should continue to be what it is, and that its inherent rational order is not self-sufficient, self-sustaining or self-explaining, while grounded in and dependent upon God's own eternal rationality and power. As such the created universe can be understood only out of its inherent contingent rationality, not through abstract necessitarian processes of thought, but through open modes of scientific inquiry in which nature is allowed to disclose and interpret itself to us in answer to our experimental questioning. Hence it was the Christian conception of the contingent nature of the material universe and the contingent nature of its unitary rational order that originally opened the way for the rise of empirical science; and it is still on the assumption of the contingency of the universe and of its rationality that all our modern empirical and theoretical science rest. They could not have arisen without it and certainly cannot continue to proceed apart from it.

It is because the universe is characterised by an immanent rational order of this kind that empirical and theoretical factors are fused with in one another at all levels, and thus interlock with one another in our scientific constructions. All scientific theories are empirically conditioned and all experimental questioning of nature is theoretically conditioned. This means that science operates through a commitment to the interior relations and rational patterns of the field under its investigation and functions under their constraint — hence it is and must be free from any constraint outwith that field. It is to nature itself, and not to any external factors, that appeal for the justification of our theories must be made, for it is nature alone that can tell us whether our scientific concepts and theories are true or false. That is the basic principle on which the Royal Society was founded, succinctly formulated in its motto, *Nullius in Verba* — on no one's word, no submission to authority. Rigorous empirical and theoretical inquiry is pursued only in strict accordance with the structures embedded in nature, and theoretical explanations are developed only under the control of those structures as they are progressively brought to light. Thus the laws of nature as formulated by science are not read into nature, as Immanual Kant thought, but are read out of nature, and are of an open-structured kind constantly revisable in terms of what may yet be disclosed from within the field of research.

We have been considering, not only the fact that our science presupposes both the rationality of nature and the contingency of nature, but also the fact that the *rationality* of nature is itself essentially *contingent.* While this radical contingency cannot be established by natural science itself, it constitutes nevertheless a *sine qua non* for its existence and continuity in the empirico-theoretical form that is now universally accepted. Moreover, ever since James Clerk Maxwell discovered the mathematical properties of light the immense advances made by natural science especially in relativity and quantum theory, and now also in non-equilibrium thermodynamics and chaos theory, have had the effect of reinforcing and even justifying this under-standing of the contingent nature of the universe and of its intrinsic rational order, because those advances are made in accord with contingency as their ultimate regulating presupposition. The point with which I am now concerned, however, is that these advances in scientific discovery arise out of ever more rigorous attention devoted to the *intrinsic* intelligibility of nature throughout the universe without imposing *extrinsic* patterns of thought on our understand-ing of it. In this way scientists have penetrated deeply into that intelligibility, and developed their theories more than ever under its control, and in greater freedom from the constraint of external factors of any kind.

If, then, we are to think of what may lie ahead in natural and in theological science, perhaps we should ask whether the conceptual interaction between them in their common acceptance of contingency may point us to areas where quite new advance will, or indeed should, be made. Because its inherent intelligibility is contingent and not open to *a priori* inspection, the universe always has the capacity to take us by surprise. However, if we are able to coordinate, at least in some measure, a theological approach and a natural scientific approach to the contingent intelligibility of the universe so that they are allowed to bear upon each other even when they appear to conflict, we may well be able to illuminate certain features in nature which demand more attention and which will prove to be significant factors in future scientific description and explanation. I believe that there are several features of this kind to which conjoint consideration should be given by natural and theological science and which hold out promise for important advance in the future. It will be sufficient for our purpose here to consider two of them.

## (1) *Real time*

Right from the start Christian theology held that time has been created out of nothing for it was brought into being along with the universe as a whole and is characterised by a contingent reality and order of its own which must be respected. It is this contingent nature of time that makes it so elusive for us to grasp. The contingency of time means on the one hand that time has no stability of its own for it is ultimately dependent on God who is eternal and not contingent, and yet it means on the other hand that time is given a reality of its own utterly different from the transcendent reality of God. As such time cannot be regarded as eternal or absolute in any way, but is to be regarded as intrinsically real, as real as anything else in the created universe and is to be understood properly out of its own intelligible nature.

However, time was not regarded in this realistic way when the foundations of modern science were laid in the 17th and 18th centuries. Thus in classical Newtonian mechanics while the concept of time was given a place in a scientific account of the system of the world, it was governed by a sharp contrast between absolute mathematical time and relative apparent time. Here absolute time was regarded as an external geometrical parameter, a static abstract standard for the measurement of velocity, and as such was clamped down externally upon relative apparent time, which had the effect of denying on-going time its contingent reality. It should be apparent that this procedure was not consistent with the scientific method advocated by the Royal Society in which appeal to external criteria was outlawed.

The promise of real change, however, was held out in the concept of the continuous dynamic field as an independent reality, advanced by Clerk Maxwell. Then there came the challenge of Kierkegaard to find a way of thinking of time and becoming in dynamic and not static categories, and the call by Bergson to return to the concept of 'real time'. With relativity theory Einstein dethroned the scientific treatment of time from its absolute status, and put forward the concept of space-time in which time is understood as an intrinsic feature of the on-going empirical world, which has since been considerably reinforced by Ilya Prigogine in his exciting development of non-equilibrium thermodynamics and the prominence he gives to the transition thermodynamical thinking requires science to make from being to becoming.[2] Moreover the finiteness of the universe already implied by the finite speed of light carried with it the finiteness of time, which together with Max Planck's constant $h$ reinforced recognition of the contingent nature of empirical reality. But in spite of all this, even with the development of four-dimensional geometries and their explanatory deployment in the relativistic conception of space-time, time itself was still given expression in traditional mathematical terms, so that as with Newton it was finally no more than an external geometrical parameter, and the concept of *real time* failed to be given proper scientific formulation.

In Prigogine's discussion of time and complexity in the physical sciences he insisted that in order to respect time as a primal fundamental feature of nature, it must be brought into scientific equations as an *internal operator*. The problem here, however, in spite of Prigogine's attempts to do this in

[2]Ilya Prigogine, *From Being to Becoming. Time and Complexity in the Physical Sciences*, San Fransisco, 1980.

his account of dynamic and thermodynamic states of matter, is that no one has yet developed a mathematics with time-related equations of the kind that can cope properly with temporal relations as internal factors in scientific theories. This is a problem that had already been anticipated by James Clerk Maxwell, when in his dynamical theory of the electromagnetic field he admittedly failed to reach a satisfactory way of coordinating location and motion in field theory — the very problem now so familiar to us in quantum theory. In spite of the incredible advance he made through his partial differential equations in the development of his field theory, he claimed that in the last resort they were 'unworkable'. What he felt was needed was a development of the kind of mathematics he discerned in Michael Faraday's concrete way of thinking in wholistic groups of continuous relations embedded in nature — 'which showed him', as Clerk Maxwell wrote, 'to have been in reality a mathematician of a very high order'. Clerk Maxwell tells us that he himself was dissatisfied with the merely analytical mathematics of the professional mathematicians, and called for a 'new mathesis', a new 'dynamical way of thinking' in mathematics, in which mathematical equations were embodied in the continuous structures of nature. He foresaw the very point to which Einstein was to give memorable expression in his statement that 'as far as mathematical propositions refer to reality, they are not certain; and as far as they are certain they do not refer to reality'.[3]

The 'new mathesis' of a dynamic embodied mathematics envisaged by Clerk Maxwell involves a revolution in scientific thinking so radical that our science has hardly begun to appreciate it, let alone enter into it. This has to do with the

---

[3]Refer to my edition of James Clerk Maxwell, *A Dynamical Theory of the Electromagnetic Field*, Edinburgh, 1982, 'Introduction', pp. 1-17; and to 'Christian Faith and Physical Science in the Thought of James Clark Maxwell', in *Transformation and Convergence in the Frame of Knowledge*, Belfast, 1984, pp. 215-237.

development of a mathematics with *real time as an internal operator* which we urgently require today, for again and again we find we do not have adequate dynamic behaviour of nature in the expanding universe. The application of mathematical equations that are not internally time-conditioned to the behaviour of nature cannot but hinder our understanding of it, especially when we find ourselves having to cope with chaotic states of affairs which may turn out to be due more to the inadequacy and distorting effects of our traditional conceptual and mathematical instruments than to baffling ways of behaviour in nature independent of our observations. Scientific exploration of the universe in its macrocosmic and microcosmic dimensions has now reached the point where Clerk Maxwell's demands must be met, and where, surely, someone will soon produce for us the new kind of embodied and dynamical mathematics which the Argus-eyed Clerk Maxwell envisaged.

Certainly an understanding of time that is derived out of its own God-given contingent reality and inner intelligibility cannot but be of considerable importance to Christian theology, in several respects, especially when time is realistically embodied in dynamical field theory. (a) It cannot but help a rigorous theological account of primary realities and events such as the incarnation and the resurrection of Christ which have space-time coordinates, as I have shown in my books *Space, Time and Incarnation* and *Space, Time and Resurrection.*[4] (b) It will enable us to clarify what is meant by history, not least in biblical interpretation, where the current appeal to historico-scientific method continues to operate with Kantian and Newtonian concepts of time governed by the scientifically discarded dualism between absolute mathematical time and relative apparent time. That dualism led to the damaging Enlightenment distinction between necessary truths of reason and acciden-

---

[4]*Space, Time and Incarnation,* Oxford, 1969; *Space, Time and Resurrection,* Edinburgh 1976.

tal truths of history which denigrated real time and failed to grasp its intrinsic intelligibility, and thereby drove a wedge between theological and scientific thinking. (c) It will be of considerable significance in helping theologians to relate divine providence to contingent events in daily our life governed by physical law; but also in enabling theologians to work out the relation between eschatology and cosmology in the expansion of the contingent universe of space and time in which God has placed us, and through which he reveals himself to us. Thus the kind of scientific advance envisaged in the application of a new mathematical way of thinking to time cannot but help theology in the future to purge itself of pseudo-scientific notions and constrain it to be more faithful to its own proper ground in divine revelation.

### (2) *Moral Obligation*
Fundamental to all our realist scientific inquiry today is the acknowledgement of the unity of truth and being, and thus of epistemology and ontology, resulting particularly from the orderly integration of theoretical and empirical factors in general relativity theory. Scientific inquiry in every field presupposes that the universe is everywhere inherently orderly, for otherwise it would not be understandable or open to rational investigation and description. Our belief in order is not something which we can prove, for it has to be assumed in all proof and disproof, and arises irresistibly as a decisive operator in our consciousness built into our minds under the impact of reality from beyond ourselves. This concept of order presupposes an ultimate ground of order transcending what we can comprehend but of which we are intuitively aware and under the constraint of which we generate order in all rational activity. Hence our rational commitment to order is an obligatory force which exercises a regulative function in all careful scientific research, judgment and explanation. Within scientific operations we cannot but submit our minds to the compelling claims of reality and its intrinsic rational order upon us, so that we

have to reckon not only with an ontological basis for knowledge but with a normative basis with which our scientific intuition resonates.

In the last analysis, then, our *scientific conscience* and our *moral conscience* are found to function together. Even in the midst of the most rigorous scientific activity we find ourselves up against a mysterious imperative that bears upon us categorically from the fundamental nature of things in the universe in deference to which we frame our understanding of its dynamic ontological structures in terms of physical law. This is more than a natural imperative for in it we are concerned with what is intrinsically and not just conventionally right: a positive obligation is thrust upon us from the ultimate ground of the rational and the moral order which gives rise to the conviction that the *is* and the *ought* are ontologically and inseparably linked together, and linked, let it be said, in a way that rules out of court the 'naturalistic fallacy' on the one hand and 'value-free science' on the other hand.

Just as in our interaction with the spatio-temporal structures of nature we find ourselves under the compelling constraint of an objective rational order of an ultimate kind which we cannot in good reason deny, so here we find ourselves under the compelling constraint of an objective moral order of an ultimate kind which we cannot in good conscience disobey. In other words, the moral order, as well as the rational order, confronts us with commanding authority and bears upon us in all our scientific activity with the force of an ontologically and rationally grounded imperative.

There are two related points in particular here which require further elucidation: (a) the relation between the rational order and the moral order in scientific inquiry; and (b) the function of a moral imperative as an internal operator in scientific determination of natural laws.

*(a) The rational and the moral order in scientific inquiry*
Einstein claimed that physical science has reached the

point where we can no longer be satisfied merely with discovering the way things actually are in the world and formulating their laws, but must press on to learn *why nature is the way it is and cannot be anything else.*[5] Thus Einstein rejected outright the idea that things are what they are for no other reason than they are what they are — they are hat they are for some reason *beyond themselves.* And so, he insisted that science must find a way of probing into the inner justification of nature's laws and bringing to light the ultimate unifying rational ground on which they rest. Hence science is bound to be concerned with how things *ought* to be as well as with how they actually are. But this, as Einstein frankly admitted, has to do with the religious basis of the scientific enterprise. Einstein's belief in a pre-established harmony between the intelligibility of the universe and the human mind and his commitment to an ultimate unifying ground of rational order (to which he liked to refer as 'God') lay behind his determination to develop a unified field theory combining all the primary forces in the universe, but that implied a recognition of the contingent nature of the universe and its unlimited range of intelligibility reaching far beyond what we can comprehend.

This brings us back to the Judaeo-Christian view that man and the created universe belong to the same contingent order so that a *cognate relation* obtains between the created rationalities of the human mind and of the natural order. In virtue of their contingent nature they both point transcendentally beyond themselves to an ultimate unitary ground of order as their source which is at once rational and moral. There are not, and cannot be, two ultimate grounds of order, the rational and the moral, but only one all-embracing ground of rational and moral order. This means that under God the rational and moral laws with which we have

---

[5]A. Einstein, 'Über den gegenwärtigen Stand der Feld-Theorie', *Festschrift zum 70. Geburtstag von Prof. Dr. A. Stodola*, Zurich, 1929, pp. 126ff.

to do within the universe are correlated in a very basic way with one another. It is understandable, therefore, that the increasing recognition in fundamental science of the contingent nature of the universe and its intrinsic intelligibility, together with the recovery of the ontological ground of epistemology, should have the effect of calling in question the artificial separation of the *is* from the *ought* carried out in the Enlightenment. Recognition of the inherence of truth and being in the nature of the contingent universe, and in our acknowledgement of it to which this gives rise, radically alters our scientific attitude to reality and reinforces the sense of moral obligation generated in the scientific mind under its compelling claims.

The inner connection between the rational order and the moral order is very evident in the simple requirement to tell the truth, for we are obliged to tell the truth about something on both rational and moral grounds. It would be irrational and immoral not to do so. Here the rational obligation which involves a relation of necessity and the moral obligation which involves a relation of freedom interlock or coincide with one another. The one takes place under the rational order. The other takes place under the compelling claims and regulating standards of an ultimate moral order. It is the increasing acknowledgement of that simple but profound sense of moral obligation toward the truth that promises to affect the whole of our scientific and moral culture in the future.

*(b) The function of a moral imperative as an internal operator in scientific determination of natural law*

It should now be clear that rather more is involved here than commitment to the reality of truth and an obligation under the compelling claims of reality to bring the truth to light and to act in accordance with it. It is an obligation devolving upon science from the ultimate ground of order to serve and even maximise order in the world: it is a moral imperative latent in reality itself in obedience to which we find ourselves striving to interact with nature not just in accordance with what things actually are, but in accordance with what they ought to be. As we have noted, there is an inner relation of a cognate kind between the two modes of compulsion or obligation for both involve a submission of the human mind to the rational and moral nature of ultimate reality so that scientific concepts and moral concepts intersect each other. We have to do here with an objectively grounded *moral factor* that is not extraneous but intrinsic to the essential nature of nature and belongs to its inherent rational order. It is a moral *ought* ontologically integrated with the commanding intelligibility inherent in the being and becoming of the universe and is included as a normative ground of order upon us. As such it must be accorded a distinct place within the regular process of scientific inquiry and critical verification as an internal operator, and cannot without violating rigorous scientific commitment be set aside and treated as only an external operator with no intelligible basis and no ontological ground in the rational order of things.

As we have noted with respect to the principle *Nullius in Verba* formulated for itself by the Royal Society, it is an essential concept of science that it operates with criteria intrinsic to the field of its inquiry and does not defer at all to any external authority. We also noted earlier that this is the way in which science through a new mathematical *mathesis* is struggling to include time as an internal operator in the formulation of physical laws. In the very same way it is incumbent on science, precisely as science, to be concerned with the ethical *ought* as an internal operator, and not as an external significance for science the more profoundly it penetrates into the controlling forces of nature, as for example in its generic engineering, when it cannot be satisfied with external criteria such as it might derive from utilitarian ethics, where what governs decision and choice has to do with an external conception of what is judged to be for the greatest good for the greatest number of people

— that is, precisely the kind of utilitarian ethics to which fascist and communist administrations have appealed in this century.

I believe that a rethinking and a restructuring of fundamental scientific inquiry and method in setting aside the rationalistic dichotomy between the *is* and the *ought*, and an inclusion of the moral imperative as an essential factor of control within the formulation of natural law is being forced on us today on every hand. This is very evident in the whole field of ecological research concerned with the conservation of the planet on which we live. But above all it is becoming more evident day by day in medical science where bioethical issues of the greatest importance for the survival of the human race have been raised. The ground for this change has already been prepared in the recovery of ontology and the role of belief in the foundations of knowledge. As that is developed through the heuristic vision of an ultimate unitary basis in the rational and moral order of things which increasingly directs the thinking of our great men of science, I believe that the prospect for the future is very promising. However, the more scientific inquiry presses to the very boundaries of being in microscopic and macroscopic dimensions alike, to the zero points of space and time where the accepted formulations of natural law become critical, and everything in John Archibald Wheeler's words becomes 'higgledy piggledy',[6] then I believe it will be the conceptual interchange between theological science and natural science, the intersection between divine and contingent symmetries, that will prove immensely significant for mankind.

---

[6]John Archibald Wheeler, 'The Oersted Lecture. On Recognising Law Without Law', *The American Philosophical Society*, Jan. 25, 1983; see also 'Law Without Law', *Quantum Theory and Measurement*, edit. by J. A. Wheeler and W. H. Zurek, Zurich, 1983, pp. 182ff.

# 4

## THE INTERFAITH MOVEMENT: THE NEXT TWENTY YEARS

### SIR SIGMUND STERNBERG

*The Templeton Prizes*

The Templeton Prizes have themselves made a big contribution to the progress of the interfaith movement. The spirit in which they are given is itself characteristic of the hopes of the interfaith movement. Some of the prize winners have made a notable contribution to it and the distinguished judges have been drawn from different faiths.

The Templeton Foundation Prize for Progress in Religion was established 'to call attention to a variety of persons who have found new ways to increase man's love of God or man's understanding of God. It seeks to help people of all nations to hear about the rich variety of new spiritual concepts and organisations'. It also helps people to see the infinity of the Universal Spirit still creating galaxies and all living things and the variety of ways in which the Creator is revealing himself to different people.[1]

This implies that no one religious group has a monopoly on God's revelation, but that God reveals himself to all people. The Templeton Foundation, however, makes clear that it does not encourage syncretism 'but rather an understanding of the benefits of diversity. It seeks rather to focus attention on the wide variety of highlights in present-day religious thought and work. It does not seek a unity of denominations or a unity of world religions: but rather it seeks to encourage understanding of the benefits of diversity'. The Prize seeks 'to stimulate the knowledge and love

---

[1] *The Templeton Foundation Prize for Progress in Religion.* ed. Wilbert Forker, Scottish Academic Press, Edinburgh 1988, p. 219.

of God on the part of mankind everywhere'.[2] The main interfaith organisations equally repudiate the idea of creating one world religion, but seek to affirm the blessings of diversity together with an overarching unity.

The Prize Winners include several people who have made a distinguished contribution to the interfaith movement. Dr Sarvepalli Radhakrishnan, a President of India, supported the creation of the World Congress of Faiths (WCF) and became a Patron of the organisation. Rve Nikkyo Niwano, the founder of Rissho Kosei-Kai has made an enormous contribution to the work of both the World Conference on Religion and Peace (WCRP) and the International Association for Religious Freedom. Cardinal Suenens welcomed the second Assembly of WCRP to Louvain, whilst Mother Teresa came to the World Day of Prayer at Assisi and also to the Oxford Conference of the Global Forum on Human Survival. Sir Alister Hardy, known for his work at the Religious Research Centre at Oxford, was a Vice-President of WCF.

Amongst the chairpersons has been Lord Coggan, former Archbishop of Canterbury, who is Honorary President of the International Council of Christians and Jews and Viscount Tonypandy, a Vice-President of the Council of Christians and Jews. The Judges have included distinguished members of all religions.

The Templeton Prize, therefore, has helped to give recognition and credence to the interfaith movement, which for many years has had to struggle to dispel the suspicion of the leaders of most religious communities and indeed also of the academic students of religions.

*Difficulties facing the interfaith movement*
This lack of support, until recent years, from religious leaders has been one of the weaknesses of the interfaith movement. As we look ahead to the next 20 years, it is sensible to look back at the 100-year history of the move-

[2]*Ibid.* p. 220.

ment to see what has been achieved and what the difficulties have been.

The 1893 World's Parliament of Religions, held in Chicago, ended with high hopes. 'Henceforth the religions of the world will make war, not on each other, but on the giant evils that afflict mankind'.[3] With these words Charles Bonney, the Parliament's President, ended the historic gathering.

Nearly 100 years later, Professor Hans Kung has voiced a similar hope, saying 'there will be no peace in the world without peace between religions'.[4]

The century since the 1893 Parliament has been one of the most bloody in human history, not only its wars but with mass extermination of the Jews and of other innocent groups of people. It has been the century of the homeless, the hungry and the refugees. Weapons of massive destruction still imperil the continued existence of human life whilst the threat to the environment endangers all life. When the Nobel Prize Winner Elie Wiessel visited Hiroshima he asked 'Am I looking at the past or the future?'

How can we ensure that Kung's hopes are not destined to the same crushing disappointment as Bonney's For certainly, the dream of inter-religious cooperation is still today endangered in many ways.

In many parts of the world there is a revival of religious extremism and fundamentalism. Dr Robert Runcie, then Archbishop of Canterbury, said in 1989 that 'the unexpected shock of the late 1980s is to discover that all over the world — in most religions and cultures — there are those who believe they should *not* tolerate others, should com-

---

[3]Quoted by Marcus Braybrooke, *Pilgrimage of Hope*, SCM Press 1992, p. 26. This book gives a history of the interfaith movement and organisations. See also *The World's Parliament of Religions*, Ed. John Henry Barrows, The Parliament Publishing Co., Chicago 1893, p. 102.

[4]Hans Kung, *Global Responsibility*, SCM Press 1991 and 'No Peace in the World Without Peace among Religions', *World Faiths Insight*, New Series 21, February 1989, p. 14.

pletely avoid those whose beliefs they consider in error'.[5]
The Chief Rabbi, Dr Jonathan Sacks, in his Reith Lectures
has said that 'the fact that the great universal monotheisms
have not yet formally endorsed a plural world is the still
unexorcised darkness at the heart of our religious situation'. The practical expression of this is aggressive evangelism and communalism. In Eastern Europe, too, new
nationalisms are often identified with religious loyalty. This
threatens the position of minorities and is fuelling
antisemitism.

There are those too who are ready to add a religious
dimension to conflicts which may have other causes. Saddam
Hussein gave a religious gloss to his invasion of Kuwait and
tried, unsuccessfully, to enlist the Muslim world in a *jihad*
against the West. President Bush assumed God's blessing
rested upon the American troops. Apocalyptic voices speak
of the next century being dominated by the struggle between the Christian West and the world of Islam. Bishop
Michal Marshall, for example, who has been asked to head
the Decade of Evangelism, has spoken of it as 'a decade of
confrontation' and said 'the call to win Islam for Christ is on
the agenda, along with other great powers, who at the
moment reject the claims of Christ'.[6]

In Northern Ireland, in the Middle East, in Sri Lanka and
many other places religious difference embitters the conflicts. In the cities of Europe, racial and religious difference
aggravate communal disturbance. The Bengali community
of East London is subject to frequent persecution and antisemitism shows its ugly face all too often.

As worrying perhaps is the fact that responsible voices are
questioning the ideal of a plural and tolerant society. The
Salman Rushdie affair was a great shock to those who
assumed that 'liberal' 'enlightenment' values were generally accepted. The novelist Fay Weldon pronounced that

[5]Robert Runcie to General Synod Summer Session 1989.
[6]*The Times*, 11.11.91.

'Our attempt at multi-culturalism is dead'.[7] The Journalist Martin Wollacott also declared that 'multi-culturalism, the liberal answer to some of these problems does not face reality squarely either. This is mainly because, in its unavoidable relativism, it devalues the cultures of both host and immigrant. To turn great universalist religions and very distinct social and cultural traditions into exhibits in a kind of common Disneyland is not the answer.'[8] This, however, is hardly a fair accusation against members of the interfaith movement who because of the depth of their own religious conviction reverence the faith of others, although it may be true of those without faith who could not see how anyone passionately believed in a religion. Hesitations about a plural society have even been expressed by the distin- guished statesman Lord Jenkins. He suggested recently that 'In retrospect we might have been more cautious about allowing the creation in the 1950s of substantial Muslim communities here'.[9]

That many speak of inevitable and continuing confronta- tion remind us how fragile is the interfaith ideal — voiced both by Bonney and Kung. The interfaith movement too is still so weak. Much of the work is still done on a voluntary basis. None of the international organisations have more than a handful of paid workers. Major religious communi- ties are still reluctant to fund the work and it is largely dependent on the generosity of a few individuals. The work is not coordinated and some international interfaith centre of information is urgently needed. Large numbers of people are in any case disillusioned with organised religion, partly at least because it seems to foment rivalry. It is questionable too how much impact religious people can have on public affairs and the search for peace.

---

[7]Fay Weldon, *Sacred Cows: A Portrait of Britain, post-Rushdie, pre-Utopia*, quoted by Paul Weller, *Outlook for Interfaith in the 1990s in World Faiths Encounter* 1992.
[8]Martin Wollacott, *The Guardian*, 15.11.91, see Weller, op. cit.
[9]Weller, op. cit.

## Keep Working Hard

Yet the only alternative to confrontation is cooperation. Rev. Nikkyo Niwano in his address accepting the Templeton Prize said that during the Second World Conference on Religion and Peace at Louvain, a British reporter asked him, 'You expend great efforts for the sake of peace, but don't you think that, so far, you have achieved very little? My reply to him was: 'I keep working as hard as I can precisely because results have not yet been satisfactory.'[10] Because the ideal is so good and the alternative so frightening, we need to go on working as hard as we can. The hope must be that the worldwide Year of Inter-religious Understanding and Co-operation in 1993, which marks the centenary of the Chicago World's Parliament of Religions, will galvanize far greater support for the interfaith enterprise.

In many ways the task for the next 20 years remains essentially the same, but involving an ever-increasing number of people, specially women. The official contact of the leaders of the world religious communities needs to be encouraged, whilst at local level those who are neighbours need help at beginning to learn about each other's faith and way of life. This involves an enormous educational endeavour. In Christian-Jewish relations, for example, there are now fine statements issued by many denominations, but all too few of the faithful know of them. They still repeat false stereotypes and teaching. It is even harder to persuade the lapsed churchgoer to revise teaching dimly remembered from childhood. Modern names of public education, such as the use of television and video, is necessary, but it is expensive.

Reading or seeing about another religion is useful. It is even more valuable to meet and get to know members of another faith. ICCJ has given much attention to such personal meeting, especially between young people, as

---

[10] *The Templeton Foundation Prize,* op. cit. p. 43.

have other interfaith organisations. Now, there is the need to open up such contacts especially with the people of Eastern Europe. Yet again travel is expensive. Many people, however, do travel for holidays or business and maybe more opportunities to learn about another culture and religion could be available to those who travel.

The theological task of defining the relationship of faith communities has to continue. Traditional teaching has often discouraged openness and dialogue, either because of fear or because of claims to unique possession of truth. For these attitudes to change the faithful need to be convinced that such openness springs from the depth of their religious conviction. Too many still feel that 'interfaith' implies indifference or relativism. The experience of many who have shared deeply in interfaith dialogue belies this. They have found their own faith deepened whilst learning respect for others. We need clear statements from religious leaders why the faithful should be reverent and open to the faith of others. We need visions of the ideal relationship of religions to each other that will command enthusiasm. Thinkers need to continue to engage with questions of truth, but increasingly this itself should become a cooperative enterprise as we begin to see the emergence of a global theology.

Practical cooperation is vital as well as the search for shared values and a global ethic. Yet before this is possible, past prejudice and persecution need to be confessed. The progress in Jewish-Christian relations, for example, has only been possible as Christians have acknowledged centuries of false anti-Jewish teaching which has contributed so much to Jewish suffering.

Hans Kung has stressed the need for a world ethic and has sketched an approach to it. Already the interfaith movements in some of their conference statements have pointed the way. A world society needs some shared values. 'Should it not be possible,' writes Kung, 'for all religions to agree at least on this basic question of criteria: what is good for human beings is what helps them to be truly human?[11] In his book *Global Responsibility* he outlines a major programme of research.

Meanwhile on a growing number of practical issues, people of all religions are learning to work together. Much of this has been made possible by the interfaith organisations, but many new groups are not so much 'interfaith' as 'multi-religious'. The Global Forum on Human Survival is one example. It brings together political leaders and spiritual leaders, together with scientists, in a common concern to save the planet. They address the spiritual, moral and practical issues related to the environment. The World Wild Fund For Nature, led by Prince Philip who has given so much support to the Templeton Award, has also encouraged members of all religions to see the spiritual dimension to ecological questions. Amnesty International involves people of all religions in the defence of human rights. There are numerous more organisations which could be mentioned and increasingly it is becoming natural for many people to work together with members of other religions. In areas of health care, social work and education, in many parts of the world, there is growing awareness that we live in a multi-religious world.

As more people of faith cooperate on practical matters, they may also wish to attend each other's worship as guests or even on occasion to pray together. Each faith community will wish to preserve its own tradition of prayer, worship and meditation. Yet occasional interfaith gatherings for prayer witness to the Oneness of God and our common humanity.

*Conclusion*
To many, difference is threatening and the assurance of salvation seems to depend upon a belief that only one's own group is in possession of it. There are those who believe that

[11]Kung, op. cit. p. 90.

the future belongs to their group, either by persuading others to join it or by their defeat. The alternative is to 'recognise the benefits of diversity'.[12] We need to do this at a religious level, as well as at other levels. Otherwise religion will be misused in support of national or communal identity.

Some years ago, the distinguished scholar Wilfred Cantwell Smith spoke of the momentous current which is about to become a flood — namely the pressure on all people of faith to become aware that they are living in a religiously plural world, 'which of course is the only world there is'. This flood, he warned, 'could sweep us quite away unless we can through greatly increased consciousness of its flow and direction learn to swim in its special and mighty surge'.[13] I believe that in the interfaith movement we are learning how to swim in this mighty and exhilarating surge, but we have to help many others learn to swim in it, lest they pull us all down into a whirlpool of conflict and confusion. As Abraham Heschel put it 25 years ago, 'The choice is to love together or to perish together'.[14]

The Templeton Foundation has made clear that progress in religion must be 'multi-faith'. Together people of all faiths can help the world to progress towards peace, justice and a worthwhile life for all.

[12]See note 2.

[13]Wilfred Cantwell Smith 'The Christian Response in a Religiously Plural World' in *Christianity and Other Religions*, Ed. John Hick and Brian Hebblethwaite, Collins 1980, p. 87.

[14]Abraham Joshua Heschel, *Israel: An Echo of Eternity*. Farra, Straus and Giroux, New York 1968, p. 186.

# 5

## EDUCATION FOR A WORLD
## OF ACCELERATING CHANGE

### THE RT. HON. LORD THURLOW

The future has been described as a 'theatre of infinite possibilities for creative action'. But the possibilities will not be enacted unless the actors are trained for their roles. We can now descry what will be needed for a fulfilled life in a fast shifting scene. We will fail our children if we persist in withholding an education that may endow them with the attitudes and mental skills necessary for what will be both a different kind of economy and society and one also that is continuously changing.

For the central feature of the world ahead is accelerating rate of change. The means of mastering a moving scenario is ability to perceive incipient processes, to understand their meaning, to plan and apply adjustments and to develop innovations and solutions to problems. These are some of the characteristics of creative thinking. The focus of the new education is therefore more powerful and wide-ranging mental skills, and, behind techniques, thinking about thinking, the cognitive sciences.*

What Alvin Toffler and others have called the Age of Information has submerged all those engaged in government, industry, commerce, scientific research, the services and professions with an overload. Knowledge, once difficult to obtain, pours out in a chaotic flood of data which we react to rather than seeking to control. The challenge is no longer how to acquire, learn and retrieve, but how to create patterns of meaning. Constructive and flexible thinking

---

*cf. Howard Gardiner's valuable survey in Science of Mind, Basic Books, 1987.

replaces absorption and manipulation of knowledge as the dominant quality of mind for control of events, exhibiting active application of intelligence, refinement of discrimination and creative generation of ideas. The Age of Cognition succeeds the Age of Information. How far do schools at present develop these mental qualities?

### Inherited Patterns

Curricula and teaching methods are a legacy of the industrial society in which modern education evolved. The framework is rooted in ancient principles which go back to the origins of Western culture in ancient Greece and which, after their application in the Roman Empire, were taken over by the mediaeval Church. 'Plato was the inventor of our secondary schools and universities . . . he did not wish his leaders to have originality and initiative'* for his ideal society was one that would never change.

Sir Karl Popper goes on to comment ironically 'I do not know a better argument for an optimistic view of mankind . . . than the fact that this devastating system of education has not ruined them.' He quotes Samuel Butler, son of one of the greatest British headmasters, as regarding the school system as 'almost deliberately made to warp and to stunt.' There has of course been much change since Butler's time, but the parameters broadly remain: for the changes have not been guided by clear objectives. Indeed, the consequences have often been worse than the methods they have replaced. This does not imply that there should now be wholesale jettisoning of traditional school subjects: on the contrary it is clearly important that the best of the past should be preserved. But new subjects must be added and teaching methods improved. Learning is, for instance, faster and more thorough if children participate actively

*The Open Society and Its Enemies, by Karl Popper, Routledge, reprint 1986.

under the motivation of innate curiosity, rather than being subjected to a receptive process that is to a great extent passive. Teachers will eventually be helped by powerful interactive video screens with which students can engage in individual dialogue. But already there are visual aids which children can themselves manipulate with the teacher adopting a role of guide and interpreter while the student retains the initiative in determining the direction and rate of learning.

## New Models

The recommendations that follow are not just theory from an ivory tower, but have been tested in practical school applications designed to develop models that can be widely applied. They are based mainly on experience of United Kingdom schools. But there is ample evidence that parallel deficiencies occur in most countries: for virtually all systems are branches from the same tree. In the U.S. there is widespread criticism of the decline of standards. In France the framework is seen to be far too rigid. In Germany there is rumbling revolt against old-fashioned teaching styles. The former empires of Britain, France, Spain, the Netherlands and Portugal covered most of the surface of the globe and each newly independent state had little choice but to continue inherited European patterns of education. Although Japan's high standards of qualifications have contributed significantly to her technological and industrial successes, her school structures appear to follow Western models. And cramming practices and exaggerated competition for examinations results may well exact a heavy eventual price in stifling independent thought and creativity. The deadly influence of Leninist doctrine imposed a mental ice age over the entire former Soviet empire and Chinese schools remain gripped in a Marxist vice.

The need for fundamental reappraisal is universal. In the intense competition that is predicted as a feature of the info-revolution, any country that remodels its schools to provide the skills that business demands to acquire a better equipped work force will enjoy powerful advantages. But the main challenge and prize lies in the realm of transmission of true values on which the health of society depends.

## The Goal

What kind of people do we wish our systems of education to produce? What mix of abilities and qualities should be the aim to evoke? Any intelligent process should have a defined object, but it is difficult to identify a clear goal of present Western schooling that relates constructively to the needs of societies in transformation. Boredom, drop-out, lack of commitment and failure are symptoms of a mismatch between classwork and the community. Much well-intentioned effort is devoted to improvement, but there has been little more than marginal adjustment within the same broad parameters. It is the nature of large bureaucracies such as state ministries of education to discourage fundamental change: so all Western countries are saddled with outmoded structures buttressed by inadequate courses of teacher training.

Meanwhile every year that passes makes the need for transformation increasingly urgent to meet the economic requirements of information technology. Alvin Toffler identifies six features of the future electronic infrastructures that will largely determine the nature of industrial economies: interactivity, mobility, convertibility, connectivity, ubiquity and globalisation. Those who work with the infrastructures will have to have matching qualities. 'When combined, these six principles point to a total transformation, not only in the way we send messages to one another, but in the way we think, how we see ourselves in the world.' Industry and commerce are already finding it difficult to hire the combination of skills they want at the same time as the pool of unemployed jobless grows. Moreover, time is running out politically: there are symptoms throughout the West of the kind of decay that generates political disaster.

Healthy democracy founders when the gap between the have and have-nots passes a certain threshold: representative institutions cannot tolerate a perpetual underclass. To quote Toffler again, 'High technology societies suffer from "an information divide as deep as the Grand Canyon"... the underclass is "a menace to social peace and ultimately a threat to democracy" . . . social justice and freedom both now increasingly depend on how society deals with three issues: education, information technology and freedom of expression. In the case of education... our mass systems are largely obsolete... A high-choice system will have to replace a low-choice system if schools are to prepare people for a decent life . . . let alone for economically productive roles . . . Education is no longer merely a priority for parents, teachers, and a handful of educational reformers, but for the advanced sectors of business as well, since its leaders recognise the connexion between education and global competitiveness.'*

*Principles of Restructuring*

Education has been concerned primarily with transmitting knowledge, scientific, humanistic, linguistic etc. But the qualities with which schools must equip the citizens of the future include, first and foremost, stronger and more varied powers of individual thinking. What is the *meaning* of the play of forces? Meaning has a dimension of value, requiring judgment. *Thinking* encompasses a broad spectrum of mental functions, many of which have been neglected in schools. The learning of analysis and reasoning, critical judgment and classification remains as necessary as in the past: there must be a firm foundation of literacy, numeracy and traditional values. But continuous and accelerating change puts a premium on creative imagination, ability to foresee new developments and to plan, lateral

---

*Alvin Toffler, Powershift, Bantam Books 1991, p. 360.

thinking to widen understanding, holistic sweep to perceive and comprehend increasing complexity, and global attitudes to grasp the interactions of a world unified by instantaneous and universal communication. At the technical level, unless children become familiar with electronic techniques and the world context, they will be to a great extent unemployable. All these needs add up to a formidable new educational challenge. How then should the curriculum be modified to supply new capacities and skills while still building on a foundation of traditional knowledge?

## A Wider Curriculum

The recommendations that follow are drawn freely from a publication* describing the practice of a small school set up to demonstrate that a wholesome innovative curriculum can successfully be combined with the traditional basic subjects. It is being validated by good academic results.

'Present education develops the critical intelligence, and discourages the generative intelligence which is more widely needed on leaving school. In many ways present methods and values are quite inappropriate for the teaching of thinking — thinking is a process and cannot be taught successfully by the content method. Teaching thinking, and even practising thinking, is difficult in knowledge-based subject areas, because speculation will always appear inferior to the actual facts which are imparted sooner or later, and because content is usually more interesting to the student than the thinking process . . . Knowledge and skills will still be vital but can no longer dominate the curriculum as before.'

We propose a division of the curriculum into five key areas.

## 1. Knowledge

Knowledge will be taught as a common core of essential facts, with the emphasis on enablement of the educational process, and of further self-study. What constitutes essential

*Education for the Cognitive Age, KET Alpha Network, Harper & Row, 1990

facts will require constant updating. Subject teaching will continue to play an important role in future curricula, but the teaching of facts will increasingly become a presentation of forms of knowledge and ways of classifying information, with new techniques for handling this.

## 2. *Skills*

The basic skills of traditional education remain essential as a foundation. They can be imparted more quickly by new methods of accelerated learning that are fun to use and enable more rapid progress. These make use of sophisticated but simple visual aids that involve the students in active participation. The classroom time saved is available for the additional subjects.

## 3. *Metaskills*

We draw a distinction between skills and 'metaskills'. Metaskills are the skills which order skills, and centre around cognitive faculties, such as analysis, synthesis, holistic vision, and judgment. As artificial intelligence and computer directed tools and services penetrate deeper into society, metaskills will be at a premium, for these are the higher order skills which characterise goal-oriented learning, and which computers will never be able to do for people.

Metaskills are the skills which are used by individuals living in a complex world in thinking, planning, learning and intellectual and moral growth. Here belong all the skills we aim to inculcate in thinking-skills courses and other crucial areas of cognitive development. These may be taught in a deliberately artificial way in order to identify the issues more clearly. They are not susceptible to content teaching, and are too important to subordinate to the teaching of knowledge, concepts or skills in traditional subject based classes. Thus we require new areas of the curriculum, with new ways of achieving the goal in conscious practice of these skills.

Central to the whole issue is the ability to increase one's rate of learning. Take-up of metaskills has to be deliberate, as in thinking-skill courses such as those introduced by the Venezuelan Government in their state schools. Metaskills are the survival skills of the future.

### 4. *Concepts*

As the domain of knowledge swells and as greater complexities are recognised, we need new concepts in order to 'make sense of the world'. Concept formation and concept review are high value survival skills in an era of continuing and accelerating change. The lynchpin of the cognitive age will be the examination and generation of concepts through individual thought and inquiry. Educationalists must formulate key concepts to inculcate and present to children as a foundation for this process.

### 5. *Values*

The most important obligation of one generation to the next is to transmit right values. Up to now these have been passed on largely unconsciously. But there is now universal questioning and conscious choice. Children will be better equipped to escape indoctrination and obsolete patterns of thought if they are able to explore value systems and to work out their implications and create new values. A large variety of values may be presented from different sources in order to help this process, but will not be taken for granted. It is no disclaimer of the moral values of Western culture to advocate understanding of other traditions.

Walter Truett Anderson, perhaps the most penetrating and perceptive exponent of the new planetary culture that is in course of gestation, regards free discussion of belief systems in schools as tending to strengthening morality. 'We see education as, among other things, a training in the skills of moral reasoning — morality not merely handed down but learned and created and recreated out of experience . . . The collapse of belief does not, it turns out, result in a collapse of morality: quite the opposite.' He sees 'a renaissance of searching for principles of life that we variously call morals, ethics, values', in 'a continued dynamic process of moral discourse and discovery'.*

The attitudes to which poets and prophets point as giving access to the highest values include wonder, worship and morality. Parents and families rather than schools have the prime responsibility for guiding children to develop such innate tendencies. School teaching of music and the arts can make a contribution. Religious education is a delicate and controversial matter for institutions: any sectarian handling of belief systems is not easy to reconcile with a school's respect for freedom of enquiry as the path to truth. The most effective means of transmitting moral values to children will always be example.

At a large boarding school for privileged boys in Gwalior in India, the whole school assembles in the fine open air amphitheatre every evening for a few minutes silence: no theme, no suggested form of meditation; simply an opportunity to be collected internally. It is said that the boys appreciate this short daily period highly. But what works in the Indian cultural tradition could not be translated to a crowded Western inner city school!

## 6. *Responsibility*

Children need to be shown how to handle their duties and their challenges effectively. A responsible attitude towards events and circumstances — which is not the same thing as a mechanical sense of duty or of self sacrifice — is a prerequisite for an intelligent decision. It begins with observation, self respect and self esteem. Children can be asked to take responsibility, within the limit of their powers, and of the teachers' overriding responsibility, which must never be abnegated. For children to learn to take intelligent

*Walter Truett Anderson, Reality Isn't What it Used to Be, Harper & Row, 1990.

responsibility for their own work, presentation, pattern of learning, and for the welfare of their friends and their surroundings, is an important part of growing up, and they need opportunities to develop this within a safe environment.

### Thinking Skills

Thinking is a range of skills, not a body of knowledge. It was suggested in the past that it could be taught implicitly in the teaching of the various classroom subjects. Recently as particular mental skills have been brought to notice, these have been seen as incidental to the learning of subjects. But thinking cannot in fact be taught effectively as a by-product of learning either humanities or science. It takes self conscious practice and deliberate application. The following can be seen to be essential components of thinking skill courses.

*Lateral Thinking.* Growing recognition has been obtained for this important technique from the excellent books and courses of Edward de Bono. Students learn to see where their thinking has been rigid and inflexible. Wider patterns are perceived, and new creative insights generated. Useful as these are they need direction to avoid scatterbrain aimlessness. Lateral thinking needs to be supplemented for purposeful learning by ways of setting goals and of forming judgments and taking decisions.

*Traditional Thought Categories.* Analysis classification, logic and linear processing towards a goal remain key skills, and must continue to be practised.

*Representation and Modelling.* Economic forecasts and war games are only two of the myriad applications of modelling that now play an indispensable part in business, commerce and administration. A model, especially computer-aided, is the only means of viewing complex issues as a whole and tracking the effects of changes. And beyond representation of particular scenarios, modelling can be used to represent a variety of types of thinking. The best route to attain a goal can be discovered by comparing different modes of thinking.

*Perception:* To some extent we all live in blinkers: most of us see only what we have become accustomed to notice and simple exercises and parlour games strikingly demonstrate the limits of our normal attention. Perception can easily be extended: accurate awareness of surroundings can be developed.

*The Cognitive Sciences:* Particular mental skills can in the latter stages of schooling be viewed together as parts of the generalised science of thought itself in all its main modes. There have been important recent discoveries about the way the mind works: some psychology, anthropology and elementary brain physiology are relevant to a balanced education, to illustrate the evolution of mind, thought, emotions, perception and learning, how they interact and the power of conditioning.

*Computer Skills:* To the basic skills of reading, writing and numeracy are now added computer literacy, programming skills, storage and retrieval of knowledge and modelling support. More and more careers call for basic computer abilities. Programming, which used to be a highly specialised expertise, is no longer difficult to learn and it is increasingly useful for practical purposes to understand the principles. New system skills in education and elsewhere require a measure of interaction with programmes. Equally, as business and government grows in complexity with instant global communication, there is both dependence on computer skills and a need to guard against misuse. Again, the field of storage of knowledge is undergoing rapid developments that are revolutionising the structuring and retrieval of data, including interactive retrieval, and multimedia display. Our relationship with knowledge is becoming dynamic, with information as a material for moulding. A new value is added to thinking as the process which acts upon information. Modelling is the art of rendering explicit mental forms that have normally been unrecognised;

and, thanks to computer support, modelling takes its place as the most effective means of gaining the power to think about arrays of factors in any complex situation or problem. Previous forecasts of the impact in education of computers and video have not been fulfilled because they have been applied within the same old paradigms: a revolution in approach must match the change of techniques.

*Mapping Your Thoughts*

A map enables you to see at a glance the features of an area and the relations between them. By making a map of your thoughts, or, say, the ideas contributed in the course of a meeting, you have a permanent visual record for further consideration. The human mind can handle only six or seven variables concurrently; this is a proven inherent limitation of our faculty of attention. There is, therefore, a strict limit to the power of traditional methods of reviewing an array of factors, assigning priorities, establishing relations and planning. Decision making is becoming more and more complex, so that new ways have to be found to handle and communicate thought. Business leaders are therefore now led for competitive advantage to adopt the new techniques of displaying thoughts in patterns or symbols, since better decisions can then be taken and greater success achieved. At the personal level the way is open to fulfilment of potential. In the evolution of culture the new methods constitute a quantum leap in means to represent thought: as reported in the preceding section, behind our conscious thoughts lie implicit and unrecognised mental maps or models, and decisions and actions are based on them.

These unconscious patterns also determine how we assimilate information. Until now our inherent mental models have been used largely automatically. Now at last they can become explicit, recognised, developed and refined to improve and speed up learning and the ability to review concepts and values. Socrates, the apostle of free enquiry, would have been in the forefront of welcoming and employing the new techniques to expand the powers of the human mind.

Cognitive mapping represents thinking by combining words and geometric shapes. The neologism 'idon' has been coined to connote the synthesis of *idea*, verbal concept, with *ikon*, an image or figure. A symbol thus constructed is drawn from both left and right hemispheres of the brain, and can express richer meaning than words, pictures or labelled diagrams by themselves. Complex structures of concepts and systems can be built up from simple single elements, using tools and techniques that are very easy to use, such as magnetic visual aids for manipulation by hand, and innovative computer software.

With such methods children learn to map knowledge and thoughts in school processes that are fun to handle. A complex whole is rapidly assimilated and hidden meaning grasped. If concepts are mapped, meaning comes to light. National or world problems can be modelled to give new insights. Children can increase their understanding by building up mental models together in class, placing idons on magnetic screens. Not only can they then learn more rapidly and effectively in school, but also they acquire the ability to handle complex challenges in later life by their capacity for clearer mental representation. Teachers have a powerful new resource for presenting knowledge: material from different sources, textbooks, electronic media, the students themselves, can be collected and represented together. The limitations of linear presentation are superseded. Cognitive mapping represents together the outer world of experience and the inner world of the mind.

## The Role of Language Studies

Language largely determines thought. Words symbolise what has been perceived and enable patterns of thought and experience to be employed for all the innumerable purposes of human life in the form of concepts. The symbol is distinct from what it symbolises, as subjective from objective: language deals with abstractions, not with experience itself, and has limitations. To understand these limitations children should learn how language works. A mother tongue is acquired in infancy from the instinct to copy, and is learned in the right brain hemisphere; it has to be learned by boys and girls as a tool rather than an inherent capacity by simple lessons on how meaning is built up and on the assumptions behind naming. But it is in the other side of the brain that a second language is learned, and the process of putting it beside the mother tongue involves the working of both brain hemispheres together. The combination probably develops an aptitude to combine them in other functions. This study gives an insight into language from a new viewpoint: it also takes a student out of the closed bounds of his home culture into the wider world beyond, a first step toward a global outlook.

*Global Understanding*

Islamic extremism highlights one of the prerequisites of future stability, that is, mutual understanding between cultures. There are always negative forces fanning flames of hatred and suspicion between neighbours, commercial rivals and different religious groups; they can be effectively countered and overcome only by increased understanding. The archaic and perverted dogmas of prejudiced mullahs can be put in perspective beside the tolerance of millions of sincere Muslims who acknowledge the broad area of shared sources and values derived from Judaism and Christianity; the great Sufi saints of medieval Islam have much to contribute to stronger and deeper moral values in the West at the present time. Time has not invalidated the Buddha's Four Noble Truths and the Eightfold Path. The Upanishads enshrine insights which the Western cultural heritage has lost sight of and is only now beginning to acknowledge. The Jewish Kabbala unfolds hidden knowledge. It is easy for rabble rousers to ignite ignorant partisan passions under the banners of distorted religious war cries, and the influence of extremists fanatics cannot be countered in the long run by repression but only by development of mutual understanding. The Templeton Prize for Progress in Religion directs a spotlight on valuable contributions of different faiths, from which follows inter-cultural understanding. Sir John Templeton built into the principles of his annual award insistence that each spiritual tradition has its own unique aspect of multi-faceted truth, and each is strengthened and not weakened by the wider vision that is gained by removal of inherited blinkers. Year by year the attention directed to spiritual commitment, service and leadership by different Christian denominations, by Hindus, Buddhists, Jews and Muslims reduces the area of misunderstanding and lays positive foundations for education in tolerance. Presentation of religious traditions in relation to each other forms part of a holistic perspective towards cultural evolution: and holistic attitudes towards the environment and ethnic groups are central to humane education. If they are to be more than an intellectual acceptance and eventually help to motivate action, holistic attitudes must be developed in children while they are very young.

### The Environment for Effective Learning

Boys and girls need self-esteem, fulfilment, security and love, all of which are essential for health and happiness. Without them there is psychological warping which may never be straightened out. Stresses and pressures that may stimulate an adult are wrong for children who are developing their capacities for feeling and thought. Happiness in school not only avoids damage but also greatly contributes to rapid progress. 'Anxiety, fear and anticipation of failure and punishment are barriers to learning.' It is important to take risks and be prepared to make mistakes, which are a way of getting feedback. And the school atmosphere outside class must be monitored strictly. The negative qualities portrayed in Lord of the Flies are not exceptional: ganging

up against the weak or abnormally gifted is a common
propensity and like all violence must not be tolerated in
leisure periods. Limited resources inevitably rule out provision of ideal conditions for the majority of children at
present but it is vital to push forward the frontier of education in pilot projects to show the way that the majority may
later follow. Revolutions start with individual leadership.
The torch is likely to be carried mainly by privately funded
schools.

### State and Private Schools

Of three main elements of education, contents, methods
of teaching and the school environment, the observations
above are directed mainly at the first area, that is, the subject
matter; but a few comments may be permitted on method
and environment, each of great importance and requiring
lengthy treatment to do them justice.

A revolution may well be approaching that could replace
current classroom practices from top to bottom: written
material will perhaps be largely supplanted by oral, books
by TV and computer screens and dialogue conducted on
radio and recorders. Screens and cassettes may no longer
be supplementary but become central to learning; but this
kind of thing may still be some way off. Most of the current
debates are concerned with the difficult immediate problems and, in large areas crisis situations, of state schools
ministering to the millions of children who have no access
to privileged private schools. Many of these problems derive
from the vast and perhaps growing numbers of girls and
boys from home backgrounds deeply discouraging to children's education — parents failing to give encouragement,
ethnic minorities with language problems and cultural
barriers, inner city poverty and squalor. Such disadvantages
are compounded by excessively large classes, inappropriate
or discredited methods of teaching, low commitment of
staff, inadequate equipment and discouraging environment. Such matters must continue to receive the high

priority they deserve, but schools wrestling with these deep-seated social challenges cannot direct energies and resources to blazing new trails. The sector that seeks to identify the kind of education that should be in future the goal for girls and boys and their teachers who can aspire to excellence will regrettably remain at any rate for a time relatively small and more specialised, though in the long run it plays a key part in determining a future of progress.

### The Need for Private Sponsorship

There is nothing difficult in releasing boys and girls from the confinement of present learning structures and endowing them with the outlook and equipment that will assure them of a constructive and fulfilling life. Practical experience has proved that a small independent school can provide the curriculum that combines the best of the past with the skills of the future. A group of parents can combine to establish the framework; advice could be made available to guide the recruitment of suitable teachers. The shared costs are not heavy; but initial help is necessary for launching.

The new education will be introduced only by private initiative: for the dinosaurs of mass education are beyond fundamental reform. Mr Nicholas Salgo of Washington has lit a beacon in his annual prize for innovation in education to be presented shortly by President Bush. What better help can grandparents give their grandchildren than contributing to attainment of right qualities? No field is more worthy of the support of charitable foundations: for the resources for making new methods available will not come from rigid state bureaucracies.

### Adult Community Education in Less Developed Countries

The priorities in the LDC's are different. It is impossible to generalise about a great variety of countries and conditions spread over vast areas of the globe with contrasting climate, resources and cultures. The following brief comments relate to those that share the predicament of a desperate race between rapid population increase and maintenance of living standards. Most of Africa falls into this group: the population of the continent, if the present widespread trend of doubling every fifteen years persists, is estimated by some experts to be likely to reach the blinding total of 4,000 million between 35 to 50 years from now. The scale of expansion is such that even the depredations of AIDS are not expected to change this prospect materially. Parts of Asia and South America face not dissimilar surges. Is it conceivably possible that resources can match rates of increase, even at standards hardly above subsistence? This is essentially an agricultural, pastoral and forestry problem, and the good news is that the results of recent research in Africa indicate that theoretically, if only the peasant farmer can adopt new and proven methods that do not involve drastic change or require large additional imputs, the race can be won.

So the problem becomes one primarily of adult education to get the potential of new techniques of cultivation through to the farmer. Since colonial days this has been the responsibility of government agricultural extension services, and subject therefore to the constraints of both limited budgets and a slow rate of impact. By the methods of the past crops could never match population numbers: much of Africa would be condemned to starve.

There is only one solution: a new form of accelerated education of the farmer and small entrepreneur is the precondition of sufficiently rapid progress. The new educational technique is already available and about to be applied in an African pilot project. It is based on the use of the simple but powerful visual aids referred to above in their school application which enable a subject to be set out in a visual form easy to grasp and transmit to others. A snowball process can be set in motion with only a modest dependence on paid instructors. The learning scheme is designed to involve participation of an entire small community, with the positive support of the elders or headmen; the learning relates to the real practical problems of the community. Wives are involved in parallel groups to learn basic practices of health and family planning. Expanded agricultural and pastoral production can by this means be balanced by progressive adoption of family planning, a two pronged attack on the resources — population challenge. Children's education must develop side by side.

The learning method can be applied anywhere, and will, it is hoped, be taken up in Asia and South American as well as Africa, specific models being modified to suit the conditions of each region. Such arrangements for community adult education are not, of course, in any way exclusive; the many existing schemes of overseas development and health assistance must be expanded as limited international resources permit, both by governments and non-governmental organisations. But accelerated community learning is likely to be the key to winning the race. No country can be raised up except mainly by its own efforts.

*CODA*

Plato prescribed principles of education for an ideal society that was designed to be static. He was reacting to the turbulence of the Athenian social system emerging from tribalism. His master, Socrates, had done all that he could to encourage individualism, insisting on free enquiry as the engine of truth. But in his disillusioned old age Plato abandoned the principle of search for truth for which Socrates had finally sacrificed his life. He withdrew into the fantasy of a changeless society, controlled rigidly from above by a self-renewing elite of elders. And his writings were so powerful that they have continued to influence schools ever since. The transmission of knowledge is even now given priority over the development of the faculties of independent thought. At last the tide is turning, and Socrates' commitment to free enquiry is again perceived as the key to advance of intelligence.

Computerisation of the economy, universal instant communication and the other aspects of the information revolution have made it unavoidable to review priorities. The revolution presents great opportunities in education, but confronts society with equally great dangers if the opportunities are not taken.

> There is a tide in the affairs of men,
> Which, taken at the flood, leads on to fortune.

It is now a matter of choice of whether to ride the wave to mastery of human destiny or to succumb to the mounting forces that threaten mankind's fragile heritage of values. The outcome will be determined in schools.

These brief notes do no more than present the views of those who speak with authority. There is no claim of originality: the author has no professional educational credentials. But a lifetime of immersion in relationships between countries in all the continents has given, if no specialised knowledge, at least a wide perspective, and confirmed the conviction that, if true values and the guidance of spiritual insights is respected, there are no problems that cannot be solved. The stakes are higher than ever before in human history: and without far-reaching restructuring of education we face catastrophe.

# 6

## EDUCATION FOR WORLD CITIZENSHIP

### UWE KITZINGER

Globalisation was the great prescription of the 1960s and 1970s. It has become the great diagnosis of the 1980s and the 1990s. But in fact it remains patchy. As always, it is those who can bring the backward sectors up to global standards and global character who, given their timing is right, will reap their reward.

Those who invested in the emerging Japanese economy in the early 1960s and 1970s brought home a lavish harvest from the seeds they sowed. Those who invested in an international education in the early 1970s rose fast to positions of responsibility in the 1980s and the early 1990s. But just as there are now all over the world other emerging growth markets to be brought up to global standards of efficiency and value added, so — indeed even more so — education is grossly unequal and absurdly provincial in character in most of the world.

'If you look for bargains all over the world, you will find more bargains, and better bargains, than if you look only in one country' is a sound prescription for financial investment. It is one whose potency John Templeton has spectacularly demonstrated in practice. If you look in more countries for models of education and paedagogic theory you will find better ideas than if you look only in one. Moreover if you educate people to operate only in one culture, you will deprive them not only of a head start in operating in a world in which work has become increasingly global in character, but also of even seeing their own culture in its distinctiveness from others. 'What does he know of England, who only England knows.'

International education, as I see it, should have as its ideal the development of world citizens. During and after the second world war, the Council for Education in World Citizenship was concerned precisely with that aim. It worked with British schoolgirls and schoolboys in their late 'teens to raise awareness of international issues. Looking beyond the end of the war it encouraged thinking about the peace to come — the creation of a strong United Nations in place of the old League of Nations, policies towards the defeated axis peoples, policies towards Europe's colonies in Africa and Asia, the re-organisation of Europe itself, ideological conflicts bound soon to sharpen between East and West, the 'four freedoms' elevated by President Roosevelt and other allied leaders to the status of peace aims: freedom of worship, freedom of speech, freedom from hunger, and freedom from fear.

The raising of awareness however has two aspects — a cognitive and a volitional one: and thus international education to develop world citizens has not only to disseminate facts and promote understanding, but must also lead to involvement in policy decisions and practical action. World citizenship is not a spectator sport. Citizenship never is: it implies participation and commitment.

We shall, in due course, come to discuss international education at the post-graduate and post-experience level, where it is discussed widely particularly in the United States at this time. But such education starts, I believe, at a much earlier time and in a much less formal way. Children today are exposed morning and evening to television and radio long before they can read. Sesame Street and quiz programmes are followed by hospital and police dramas, and murders in detective stories by terrorism, sabotage, riots and civil wars on the news. To separate fiction from reconstruction, and reconstruction from reality is not always easy for a child. But thanks to technology the events in another town are as real as — but no more real than — the events half a world away. An explosion in Ulster, a fire in Los Angeles, the siege Sarajevo and a protest in Bangkok come over with equal immediacy. Combined with a good school atlas the material is there for education in world citizenship to start at a pre-school age and in the home itself.

The material, that is, for the cognitive aspects. Understanding, sympathy, and a feeling of involvement do not follow automatically. Our four-year-old grandson played with guns happily in spite of discussions of the horrors of war in Eastern Europe and the former Soviet Republics until, one day, he saw hundreds of teddy-bears arrive in the dining-room and understood that hundreds of children had lost their toys, their homes, and often their parents. That was when he began making suggestions on how to end the war: send out hedgehogs so the soldiers can't march — but then they might shoot the hedgehogs; fill the lorries returning from the delivery of relief supplies with their bullets, so they can't shoot any more. . . .

Even in the younger forms at school age, awareness of the wider world and of its problems can be fostered by motivated infant and elementary school teachers. In Britain as I write scores — probably hundreds — of school classes are filling care parcels in shoe boxes with toys, chocolate and clothing and with their photos, names and addresses to send to refugee children in or from Dubrovnik; scores of children have had heart-rending simple letters of thanks describing the refugees' conditions of life, fears and hopes, and now want to remain in touch with 'their' Croatian families. Such early lessons in practical European solidarity and world citizenship have every chance of remaining with these children for life.

At the secondary level, human sympathy can start to be supplemented by institutional considerations. If a 'national curriculum' means a concentration on British geography, British history, English literature and British institutions it is, these days, not much more justifiable than the French system by which, only a few decades ago, West African and Vietnamese children learned all about 'nous les Gallois' and the mistresses of 17th century French kings. Britain is condemned these days to ever increasing dependency on

the rest of the world, and has to take an increasing number
of decisions as a part of the European Community: the
history and institutions, mind-sets and problems of her
partners in that Community are now as relevant as — or
rather, are now more relevant than — those of Wales and
Scotland and Ireland have in the past been to the English.
The same of course goes for the other members of the
European Community.

Given the world responsibilities inescapably thrust upon
the United States, an American-centred education would
be equally out of place today — and so would a purely
European-centred education in Europe. World economic
forces and religious and ideological movements, problems
of hunger, disease, catastrophes and the fast deteriorating
environment need to be addressed as part of the prepara-
tion for the right to vote and the other aspects of adult
citizenship. Wars such as that against Iraq may concentrate
the mind wonderfully, but they do so too late. Most secondary school children get an idea of the place of their city or
state in the country, but they need to get an at least equally
clear idea of their country's place in the international
system, and of that evolving system itself. We really need to
spend more effort on devising European and world school
curricula than on perfecting or standardising a national
one.

But again it is not only a matter of classroom knowledge
— it is also a matter of personal experience and engage-
ment. As populations come to be slightly more intermixed,
with migrant and refugee families added to a population in
which colour and ethnic discrimination are, one must
hope, gradually being eroded, classrooms are becoming
culturally less monochrome and diversity will become more
of the norm. When at school in Jamaica my daughter was
unable to answer the question whether a friend invited for
her eighth birthday party was black or white: 'But I didn't
look at her colour, Mummy, I looked at her.' School-fellows
of different backgrounds are increasingly enlarging chil-

dren's viewpoints and bringing a more global perspective into their everyday lives. Exchanges of school-teachers between countries, and family exchanges at least in the holidays if not in term-time are obvious further means of bringing home to secondary school children the diversity of national cultures and the complexities of international relations.

The tertiary level of College and University education catches a much smaller proportion of the population. Those who do not go on to participate in it, however, should not regard their education for world citizenship as completed. The mobility of labour now formally guaranteed by the legislation of the European Community facilitates a period of work in another country, learning — the best way possible — another language, and beginning to understand the cultural assumptions of other peoples.

Nor need such early foreign work experiences be confined to Europe. Opportunities to serve in Africa, Asia or Latin America have opened up over the past decades for youngish men and women once they have mastered appropriate useful skills. Such overseas work experience may indeed prove far more formative, constructive and in every sense more rewarding than a straight continuation at College of the rather artificial life of more lessons, reading and homework and the semi-sheltered youth culture social life surrounding them for another three or four years after the age of 18. A new generation of employers less preoccupied by degrees, diplomas and certificates and with a more acute interest in personal calibre, breadth of view and initiative, is coming to respect such curricula vitae while on the other hand significant proportions of recent College and University graduates find it difficult to avoid the dole queues. Perhaps to inspire and facilitate such overseas practical experience and practical use to the host country would be the most cost-effective form now of developing education for world citizenship.

Increasingly at least in the United States a period of time — often a year abroad — is being built into the more formal institutionalised patterns of national systems of tertiary education. Most of these schemes, being integrated into a formal learning curriculum, leave the students abroad essentially as spectators or voyeurs, watching but not contributing to the life of their host country. Many of them also suffer badly from only providing essentially group experiences — meaning that even when physically abroad there are plenty of young people speaking one's own language and sharing one's own assumptions all around. Such cacooned or at least mediated group tours even if they last nine months are a poor substitute for immediate individual immersion in another language and another way of looking at life. They are better than nothing, but the resources expended on them might be more productively employed in organising less supervised dispersal.

There is however another form of tertiary education: one which escapes national systems altogether. The traditional and mediaeval Universities whether in Bologna or Salamanca, Paris or Oxford were genuine Universities, recruiting their teachers and their students from all over Christendom (and sometimes even from the Arab world). They had the advantage of existing in the context of a common classical culture, a common religion, and largely analogous living conditions even if highly diversified regional variations. But the nation state had not yet drawn hard and fast boundaries around perceptions and systems: so there was nothing surprising or strange—indeed nothing that seemed remarkable at the time — in the best teachers and students congregating from all over the European mainland and its surrounding areas in the common pursuit of a single corpus of classical and religious, philosophical and later scientific knowledge.

Some of that cosmopolitan unity survived into the 18th and 19th centuries. Since then, in the 19th and 20th century when few systems escaped becoming pervaded by national governments, national economics, national preoccupations and stereotypes and blinkers, frontiers have come to impose themselves heavily and divide the processes and content of education. There is today therefore every reason — indeed an urgent need — to revive the concept of truly international or indeed supranational methods and institutions of education.

At the post-graduate level, many Universities all over the world — nowhere more so than in the United States — can now boast of a fairly international mix of students, though in almost all of them the predominant majority is drawn from the country in which the institution finds itself. To a much lesser extent American Universities have been able, since the 1930s, to give refuge to or indeed attract with favourable working conditions high-level teachers from some other parts of the world. Few however have gone beyond that in the scope of their internationalisation.

We all know that resources are limited, and in practice financial and physical and above all personnel constraints will prevent us from attaining the optimum. That however is no reason for defining what the optimum might look like, and then going back to check how far different aspects of it may or may not in different circumstances be attainable. What then would be required for a truly international education in the future?

Institutions do in practice have to have a local habitation within a national culture. It is not a bad idea however to place them at a crossroads of culture — be it Bruges, Strasbourg or Geneva in Europe, Hong Kong in Asia or analogous locations elsewhere. A number have opted for multiple locations — like the European business school with campuses in four countries and the obligation to spend an academic year in at least three of them. If neither is possible, then a quiet location in which the institution can make its own life relatively isolated from the dominant national environment — Fontainebleau rather than Paris, Florence rather than Rome — could be a third way of attempting to mitigate the problem.

In the second place, it would seem essential that the head of any institution aspiring to offer international education should be of a nationality other than the host country. She or he will need to be assisted ably by some local nationals on the administrative staff to ensure the bureaucratic liaisons that may be required with the local and national authorities and the local community. But both in the external roles incumbent on any head of an educational institution and in the at least equally crucial internal academic and cultural leadership tasks, her or his job will be to balance the local national influences by representing a contrasting network and contrasting traditions. It is difficult to overestimate the role played in setting the tone and the targets of an educational institution by a purposeful leader: and without purposeful leadership no international educational institution can ever get established.

Thirdly there occur all the problems of recruiting a truly international academic staff. It is easy to say 'we have 12 nationalities on our staff of 60' but if 49 of them come from one country, particularly if it is the host country, that is not and most likely never will be an international institution. Given the starkly contrasting remuneration levels and working conditions in the academic communities of different countries to build an international faculty is difficult at the best of times, and can probably best be achieved by whipping up enthusiasm for an essentially new, clearly defined and avowedly idealistic educational venture. It may be even more difficult to achieve an internationally representative or even an adequately heterogeneous faculty if one is building on an already established national institution within a national tradition and framework and most likely therefore with a fairly homogenous original staff, many of whom would have to be replaced regardless of their merits if one is to achieve an adequate international mix.

What goes for a faculty mix goes also for the student body. You may have 30 nationalities among 300 students, but if — to take an extreme example — some 200 of them come

from one country, and about three students from each of 29
other countries spread over the rest of the world, you do not
have an international student body: what you do have is a lot
of foreign students, and that is an entirely different thing.
I suspect that a fifth of staff and a fifth of students from any
one country — and not from the country where the institution is located — is really the maximum proportion toler-
able if you are aiming at an international education for
global citizenship.

The next requirement is a curriculum designed for
multicultural students in an intercultural setting. To expand on that essential would in itself take a fair number of
lengthy contributions to a heavy tome reflecting different
cultural starting-points and perspectives. Indeed, it would
almost be a denial of my main thesis for any one person,
inevitably trapped to some extent in one or at most two
cultural traditions, to try to go very far in attempting to
frame such a curriculum. It would be the first task of the
multicultural staff — and an investment of possibly even
several years of their time — to collaborate in reflecting on
the manifold considerations relevant to such a plan of
studies. But it can be done, and in places it has been. Indeed
in professional schools it is not too difficult: over the years
the European Institute of Business Administration INSEAD
has achieved remarkable strides in creating an intercultural
management studies programme. Lawyers and economists,
anthropologists and political SCIENTISTS would also find
the task not too daunting. Literature and history may
require a good deal of work that is yet to be accomplished.
But if a general all-round education is the aim, the integration of subjects and their compression would become very
difficult, and a variety of rival experiments therefore particularly desirable.

The design of the curriculum would condition the production of suitably intercultural teaching materials appropriate to the disciplines in question. The aim of such
teaching material has to be twofold: one, to highlight

contrasts by comparisons the other, to illuminate international or intercultural interactions. The two aims would demand different types of material. The first might, in a business school for example, set a quantitatively identical micro-economic problem of a firm facing contraction in its business in a Japanese, an American, a French, a Hong Kong, and a Scottish setting to illustrate differences in domestic attitudes, legislations and organisations. The second might follow the business methods of a multinational firm in its adaptations to different markets and its utilisation of the very differences between them. In politics comparisons of electoral systems between countries would serve the first, analyses of different types of inter-governmental and supranational organisations alongside traditional multilateral diplomacy would serve the second purpose.

Next there are the issues of paedagogic methods. The difference between the individual home tutor that was the privilege of the nobleman of the past and the present system of collective school and University education is the process of socialisation within a peer group added by the latter. In British schools typically it is the games programme and the extra-curricular activities which are designed to foster such socialisation. Within the academic curriculum it is only the odd project that fosters this essential respect of education. However in law schools and business schools particularly at the post-graduate level the moot and the case study have assumed an important socialising function of this kind. I believe that for the future of international education, this model is of particular importance.

This teaching method — or, to characterise it better, this learning method — relies heavily on group work. It thus stands in marked contrast to the highly individualised and normal University method of pitting each against each in competition for the best places on a ladder of individual success or failure. It recognises that in real life we are dependent largely on each other, and that how we fit into and how we contribute to group endeavour will, for most of us, determine our social usefulness and the balance of satisfactions as against stresses that we experience in our work. In this respect it has advantages of its own, quite apart from whether or not it is used for particularly international education.

Even within a purely monocultural context students have much to teach each other, particularly if they come from different academic disciplines or life experiences. To take but one example, in management studies the mathematician, the sociologist, the economist, the historian, the political scientist, the anthropologist, the lawyer, the biologist and the engineer will have very different approaches to the study of business organisations.

But there are things that students will not teach each other, but which they will learn from each other all the more. Especially if competition is introduced between groups and there are tough time-limits which impose calculated strains and stresses into the group process, individuals will have to learn how not only to put up with each others' views and indeed with each other as personalities, but also how to use diversity of knowledge, diversity of outlook, diversity of talent constructively through a group process towards a common goal.

If this is so within a purely national context, it is truer still when it comes to education for world citizenship. The added dimension in multicultural work — and it is a very valuable addition indeed — is that students from the widest possible different national and cultural backgrounds working together on tough problems will learn an enormous amount from each other. They will learn both about each others' culturally induced premises and presuppositions, prejudgments and prejudices, and also about different patterns of interpersonal interaction endemic in or insidiously inculcated by different cultures.

The secret in good international education therefore is to select by computer small working groups for maximum personal, cultural and professional incompatibility. Then each group has to be set tasks with salient international and intercultural dimensions that will elicit their differences to the utmost — tasks on which they will have to collaborate to achieve success in competition with the other similarly heterogeneous groups. The result should be not only that students become aware of differences, not only that they learn how to surmount them, but also, thirdly, that each student takes stock of the relativity of her or his own preconceptions stamped on them imperceptibly by their own society and their particular positions within it.

Many of these preconceptions are imbedded in the students' native languages, not only in the wise saws and turns of phrase, the metaphors and the analogies current in their cultures, but in the very modes of expression and the very vocabulary used. Any translator knows the difficulty of rendering abstract — particularly emotive — concepts into a language far from the culture in which the concept evolved. We are becoming familiar now with a wide variety of words of that kind which have been found simply untranslatable, whether from the German, the French or the Japanese. It is therefore incumbent upon any international education to insist on students learning — to speak, to listen, to write as well as to read — at least one foreign language. No institution can any longer be taken seriously in this field without a properly equipped language laboratory. But in the end the language requirements also imply an extended soujourn in at least one foreign country, with real immersion and working involvement in its daily life.

It is a very serious impoverishment for the English-speaking nations that wherever a television reporter may roam, in China or Peru, Iran or Azerbajan, he will find people articulate in English to speak to camera. It is an even greater disadvantage to the Anglo-Saxon traveller that wherever he goes, hotel staff and travel agents, airline clerks and guides will dispense him from the trouble of learning any other language. In commerce and politics it is also a major disadvantage that whatever we say to each other in print or on the air, our views and reactions, our problems and our plans are perfectly transparent to the rest of the world, while Serbs and Japanese, Iraquis and Ukrainians have the privilege of being far more inscrutable, far less internationally overheard in practice.

If the Dutch can learn three other languages because they can hardly move 100 miles from home without having to speak one of them, it should not be beyond the wit of Anglo-Saxons to speak one or two other languages than English. It is a matter of starting early also — and especially — on that aspect of international education. Nations would do well to have policies of raising balanced corps of people who would speak different languages: for commercial purposes it would be less than optimal suddenly to have a spate of Mandarin speakers if there is no one to sell in Korean, Hindi or Arabic to customers in those markets.

This now becomes particularly important as the stock-in-trade of international commerce turns more and more from hardware to services. Services largely take the form of knowledge and know-how and therefore it is not only how you sell but actually what you sell and how it is perceived in your market that is dependent on your linguistic proficiency and on your cross-cultural interpersonal skills.

In designing an institute of international studies there are two further aspects on which I would lay stress. The intense and at times painful but overall exhilarating processes of multicultural education create very strong bonds between fellow students, and a high degree of cohort loyalty. It is up to the students themselves — but up to the institution to help them — to remain in touch, and thus to continue these intercultural interchanges for the rest of their careers, indeed lives. Some of these institutions maintain alumni clubs in various countries, publish alumni address books, and arrange 'home-coming' weekends for families so that the links forged at the institution often continue into another generation.

I believe that international education — as indeed increasingly most other forms of education — can no longer depend on the clockwork mouse theory: that once people have been wound up and acquired a stock of knowledge and skill in their twenties, they are by that simple early priming sufficiently equipped for the rest of their careers and the rest of their lives. The greater the acceleration of change in the environment and the faster the advances in knowledge, the more urgent the need for periodic updating of knowledge and re-treading of skills. Perpetual learning and re-learning has become a duty of all who aspire to play a responsible part in the world of today as well as that of tomorrow.

The need for continuing education therefore applies at least as much to international as to almost any other form of education. It is thus fitting that, at Oxford, Templeton College more than any other institution specialises in this updating and re-treading of professional skills for men and women from many far-flung parts of the world who are already well advanced on successful careers.

The final point I wish to make applies increasingly to all institutions of education, but most especially to any that are seeking to change their own character — for instance from an essentially national to an international vantage-point. Education is a naturally conservative industry, to which teachers tend to co-opt their clones. Equally, changing a curriculum, it has often been said, is more difficult than moving a cemetery. Education is also a highly protected industry: it is protected by language barriers and habits of thought, by inherited prestige and most often by public financing and by rationed capacity. It is an industry dominated by restrictive practices of the producers, with all too little input by the ultimate consumers of its work. It does not easily undertake from within the sort of reforms which the changes in the world about it make more and more urgent.

But as war is now a matter too important to be left to generals, so education is now too crucial a determinant of our society's future to be left to the educators. Particularly if education is to become more international there is a strong case not only for more active and involved, committed and outspoken lay Trustees, Councils, University Courts and Governors, but also for more internationally composed bodies of that kind in the future. Their job will be either to put the necessary dynamic under the failure of nationally ossified institutions and to refuse the various 'internationalising' fig-leaves which we have seen donned over the past few years by some of the leaders among them, or else to by-pass the existing tradition-bound institutions — it may be just too difficult really to change them — and instead start new ones, from scratch.

# 7

## THE FUTURE OF THEOLOGICAL EDUCATION

### THOMAS W. GILLESPIE

One key to excellence in private institutions of higher education is a board chairman who sees to it that the school has the financial resources that enable the administration and faculty to achieve the mission goals they have been assembled to pursue. John Marks Templeton fulfilled this role at Princeton Theological Seminary during his thirty-seven-year trusteeship, twice serving as chairman of its board for six-year terms. The legacy of Sir John's leadership is attested by the remark of Dr Robert Wood Lynn, then the vice-president for religion at the Lilly Endowment, that Princeton Seminary is 'the only adequately capitalised theological school in the world'. Whether or not the institution itself merits its reputation for excellence, it is certain that provision for such a possibility has been made in no small measure through the stewardship of resources exercised by this devout and visionary layman. The present essay represents a modest expression of gratitude to Dr Templeton for his extraordinary service to one school, among many, that has a major stake in the future of theological education in the United States.

### I

Given the social disestablishment of Protestantism and the cultural relativisation of Christianity that has occurred in the United States during this century, it is necessary to ask whether theological education has a future in such an environment. For theology is the peculiar responsibility of particular faith communities. As my colleague Daniel L. Migliore explains:

theological inquiry does not arise in a vacuum. It is not built on amorphous religious experiences or on the pious imaginations of isolated individuals. On the contrary, the work of theology is inseparably bound to an identifiable faith community that worships God, attends to Scripture and its account of God's work and will, and engages in manifold ministries of education, reconciliation, and liberation. In short, theological inquiry requires continuing participation in the common life of a community of faith, prayer and service. Apart from such participation, theology would soon become an empty exercise.[1]

When the future of such communities is at risk, therefore, the task of theology, as well as its educational mission, is equally so. In the face of the continuing decline in membership and influence of the so-called mainline churches in the United States, what basis is there for affirming a future other than one of increasing marginalisation for their respective theological enterprises and the educational institutions that serve this purpose?

The answer, of course, depends upon how one understands the dynamics of history. Our modern tendency is to read the future as the outgrowth of social, economic and political energies operative in the present. Sociologist Peter Berger, for example, contends that the twenty-first century is already here in the active and latent forces of our society. The flowers of tomorrow are present in the seeds of today. This truism does not warrant the inference, however, that the future can be predicted merely by projecting vague trends forward in time. History is full of surprises. Who among us could have forecast a decade ago the incredible collapse of state socialism in eastern Europe, the reunification of Germany, and the disintegration of the Soviet Union? Even so, the future of faith communities in the United States defies assured prediction on the basis of their present social status.

---

[1]Daniel L. Migliore, *Faith Seeking Understanding* (Grand Rapids, Michigan: William B. Eerdmans, 1991), xii.

Further, the faith that informs Christian communities gives them reason to believe that the Church, although vulnerable to cultural influences, is not dependent upon such historical forces for its existence but upon the transcendent purpose and power of the God who continually creates it through the gospel of Jesus Christ. The point is illustrated by the experience of the Church in mainland China. Driven underground by the ruthless oppression of the Communist state and cut off from all contact with the outside world, the Church in China disappeared from view for four decades. Many western observers believed it had been eradicated totally. Yet, with the recent changes in the political atmosphere of the People's Republic, the Church has resurfaced with membership growth numbers that boggle the mind.

The basis of this confidence in a future for the Church is based upon what Canadian theologian Douglas John Hall calls its 'foundational past', that history attested in the scriptures of the Old and New Testaments. He writes:

> Unlike some varieties of religious belief, Christianity contains a vital and indispensable historical component. The character and will of the God in whom Christians trust is manifested, first of all, not in individual religious experience but in a sequence of historical events, the culminating moment (*kairos*) of which, for the *Christian* side of biblical faith, is the event of the Christ. In the sequence of occurrences surrounding this central *kairos*, including the long march of the people of Israel, the God in whom the disciple community believes is self-revealed. All subsequent revelation is 'dependent' in relation to this 'original revelation'; that is, so long as a community designates itself 'Christian', it is beholden to the scriptural testimony to the foundational historical events which establish the fundamental character of Christian belief.... Like all history, the biblical record consists of event plus interpretation; and here the primary interpretational element or hermeneutic is faith — faith in God as the one acting in and through this history for the world's redemption.[2]

[2]Douglas John Hall, *Thinking the Faith: Christian Theology in a North American Context* (Minneapolis: Augsburg, 1989), pp. 257-58.

Anyone grounded by faith in this 'foundational past' has reason for believing that the future is the time of God's continuing redemptive labours. In this future the Church will continue to play an instrumental role. Not least among its various tasks will be that of theological reflection and education.

## II

One cause of the current malaise of the churches in the United States is the exile imposed upon faith and theology by western intellectual culture. Generally since the Enlightenment and the subsequent rise of modern science, each in its own way exercising a powerful hegemony over the nature and conditions of authentic human knowledge, theology has been marginalised in the public forum. It is the common wisdom of our secularised society that science *knows* while theology merely *believes*. The knowledge claims of theology are viewed in public opinion as matters of *personal opinion*. In such a cultural milieu it has become ever more difficult to speak convincingly of theological conviction in terms of truth.

Theologians, seeking to make a case for Christian belief in accordance with the accepted 'public criteria' of knowledge in our secular culture, have tended understandably to devote their attention more to the issue of method (how to do theology in a scientific manner) than to the constructive task of articulating afresh the theological content and the ethical implications of the Christian faith (actually doing theology). The result, as Jeffrey Stout sees it, is that theology has 'lost its voice, its ability to command attention as a distinctive contributor to public discourse in our culture.' Sensitive to the dilemma of contemporary theologians — either turn their backs on the traditional sources of theology in order to be heard by the educated public or vice versa — Professor Stout notes nevertheless that 'preoccupation with method is like clearing your throat: it can go on for only so long before you lose your audience.'[3]

[3]Jeffrey Stout, *Ethics After Babel* (Boston: Beacon Press, 1988), p. 163.

It is my conviction that we are presently living in a time of revolutionary change in our intellectual culture that will deliver theologians from the horns of their current dilemma. Theology will recover its voice in the future as theologians and the educated public become aware of the newly emerging understanding of the nature and conditions of human knowledge. These developments will not vindicate the truth claims of theology, but they will allow them to be made on a level playing field for the first time in three centuries. The changes I have in mind are evident in the works of scientist Michael Polanyi and philosopher Hans-Georg Gadamer.

In his major book on a post-critical philosophy of knowledge, Polanyi argues the thesis that all knowledge, including that of science, is 'personal'.[4] By that he does not mean that knowing is merely a subjective act that is unrelated to and uncontrolled by what is known (objective reality). His point is rather that the knower plays an active, not a passive, role in constituting knowledge. As human beings, he writes, 'we must inevitably see the universe from a centre lying within ourselves and speak about it in terms of a human language shaped by the exigencies of human intercourse. Any attempt rigorously to eliminate our human perspective from our picture of the world must lead to absurdity' (p. 3). This recognition of the active role of the knower in any act of knowing discredits effectively the old scientific ideal of pure *objectivity* in authentic knowledge, no matter how much lip service scientists and scholars continue to pay it. The role of the knower in natural science is evident from the necessity of formulating *theories* in order to discern the rationality of nature that is hidden behind empirical data. Theories are indeed tested for their value against the reality under investigation, but they remain the contribution of the scientist nonetheless.

[4]Michael Polanyi, *Personal Knowledge: Towards a Post-Critical Philosophy* (Chicago: The University of Chicago Press, 1962). Page (p. ) references to citations are given in the text above within parentheses.

Because human knowledge is 'personal', Polanyi argues that it necessarily includes such components as *passion, commitment,* and, yes, *belief.* Citing with approval St Augustine's maxim 'Unless you believe, you shall not understand,' Polanyi contends that in a formal sense belief is foundational for knowledge. It is the loss of this insight that characterizes modern thought since the Enlightenment. By thus repudiating one of its two cognitive powers, the modern mind not only reduced belief to the status of subjectivity (opinion) but lost its capacity to accept its own statements as matters of belief. The *personal* nature of knowledge, however, requires a fundamental change of attitude. As Polany puts it:

> We must now recognise belief once more as the source of all knowledge. Tacit assent and intellectual passions, the sharing of an idiom and of a cultural heritage, affiliation to a like-minded community: such are the impulses which shape our vision of the nature of things on which we rely for our mastery of things. No intelligence, however critical or original, can operate outside such a fudiciary framework (p. 266).

This identification of belief as 'the source of all knowledge' and its location in a 'fiduciary framework' constituted by our 'cultural heritage' and a 'like-minded community' leads naturally to the complementary work of Hans-Georg Gadamer, who seeks to reclaim the essential role of *tradition* and *authority* in historical human knowledge.

*In Truth and Method,* Gadamer critiques the modern ideal of knowledge untainted by prejudice as an Enlightenment prejudice.[5] To the rationalists of the Enlightenment, *prejudice* meant an 'unfounded judgment' based uncritically upon such heteronomous influences as ecclesiastical tradition and authority. Without denying that prejudices can be false, Gadamer recognises them as 'pre-judgments' (beliefs?) that function *provisionally* in every human effort to

[5]Hans-Georg Gadamer, *Truth and Method* (New York: The Seabury Press, 1975), pp. 239-40.

understand anything. The reason for this is that human life is historically and culturally conditioned. 'Long before we understand ourselves through the process of self-examination,' Gadamer points out, 'we understand ourselves in a self-evident way in the family, society and state in which we live' (p. 245).

Here Gadamer challenges the Enlightenment vision of a universal reason, free from the distortions of historical and cultural influences, on the ground that it is simply untrue to the actual human condition. Because human life exists only at particular historical times and within various cultural traditions, Gadamer infers that 'the idea of an absolute reason is impossible for historical humanity'. Reason functions 'only in concrete, historical terms,' that is to say, 'it is not its own master, but remains constantly dependent on the given circumstances in which it operates.' The truth is that 'history does not belong to us, but we belong to it' (p. 245). Thus 'we stand always within tradition,' and this historical location conditions all human knowledge including that of science (p. 250-51).

By its own prejudice against prejudice, the Enlightenment deprived tradition of its authority, its ability to communicate authentic knowledge. Oppressed by this prejudice, Christian theology has been unable since to appeal persuasively to the proper source of its knowledge claims (its authority) in that part of the ecclesial tradition identified as sacred scripture. Gadamer acknowledges that when tradition is granted an authority that excludes critical appropriation, it can become indeed a source of unfounded prejudices. 'But this does not exclude the possibility that it can also be a source of truth,' he argues, 'and this is what the enlightenment failed to see when it denigrated all authority' (p. 247). For Gadamer, the authority of tradition resides in its ability to communicate truth. Authority is based 'not on the subjection and abdication of reason, but on recognition and knowledge'. Properly understood, authority 'has nothing to do with blind obedience . . . but rather with knowledge' (p. 248). The point is that tradition can and does teach us truth that is unavailable elsewhere, and when its truth is recognised, tradition exercises its innate authority.

It is important to note that this critique of the knowledge ideal spawned by the rationalism of the Enlightenment and the empiricism of modern science is being conducted by scientists and philosophers, not theologians. I consider the intellectual trend of this criticism irreversible, and when its implications are recognised by the educated public, theology will recover its voice in American society. Whether its voice will be heard in the public arena is uncertain, but it will not be possible in the future to dismiss theology in principle because its truth claims include *beliefs* that are mediated by a *tradition* that exercises *authority* by communicating knowledge. The renewal of theology will in turn, through the theological education provided to the ecclesial leadership of the future, enable churches to recover confidently their faith in the God who makes himself known to the world by means of their 'foundational past'.

### III

Related to theology's loss of voice in the modern world is the alleged loss of a unifying subject matter in theological education. At present, the endeavour of theological seminaries and divinity schools to educate ecclesial leadership is conceptually in a state of ferment if not turmoil, according to Kenneth A. Briggs. Reporting on this discussion for the Lilly Endowment, he identifies it as 'this century's most searching examination' of the aims and purposes of theological education. Briggs correctly perceives that the fundamental question is 'what exactly is "theological" about theological education?'[6]

---

[6]Kenneth A. Briggs, 'Probing the "whys" of theological study,' *Progressions: A Lilly Endowment Occasional Report* 4/2 (April, 1992), p. 2.

The opening shot of this conflict was fired across the bows of theological schools by Professor Edward Farley in his seminal study *Theologia; The Fragmentation and Unity of Theological Education.*[7] His central thesis is that theological education is characterised today more by fragmentation than unity. Farley's harsh judgment is that the 'typical product of three years of seminary study is not a *theologically* educated minister'. 'At its very best,' he continues, 'a theological education is only the beginning of a career-long discipline, and it is just this continuing "study of theology" which does not occur' (p. 4).

At fault is not the student but the curriculum. Farley observes:

> Education in the theological school is not so much a matter of 'the study of theology' as a plurality of specific disciplines, each with its own method. These areas of study ('sciences', disciplines, courses, catalogue fields) are offered without any highly visible rationale which clarifies their importance and displays their interconnection (p. 2).

The plurality of disciplines with their respective methods to which Farley refers include *history* (in relation to biblical studies and church history); *philosophy* (in relation to theology and homiletics); *psychology* (in relation to pastoral care and Christian education); *sociology* (in relation to church and society studies); *communications* (in relation to instruction in speech); and *management* (in relation to church administration). The outcome of such an educational experience, Farley concludes, is anything but surprising: 'Theological education in so far as it is the 'study of theology', a unitary, coherent study, is self-education, a synthetic accomplishment of the occasional individual student' (p. 5). Put simply, it is up to the students to make sense out of the plethora of courses that constitute a degree programme at their respective schools.

---

[7]Edward Farley, *Theologie: The Fragmentation and Unity of Theological Education* (Philadelphia: Fortress Press, 1983).

How then has theological education painted itself into such a corner? Farley addresses this question from a historical perspective, identifying three formative periods in the development of theological education in the United States: 'the period of pious learning (divinity), the period of specialised learning, and the period of professional education' (p. 6). In the initial state, *divinity* denoted 'not an objective science but a personal knowledge of God and the things of God in the content of salvation.' Here the study of theology was 'an exercise of piety, a dimension of the life of faith' (p. 7).

Shortly after the founding of theological seminaries as post-baccalaureat educational institutions, the second period of *specialised learning* was initiated by those early faculty members who had studied in Germany and, upon their return, introduced the theological encyclopaedia model of the European universities with its standard fourfold division of theological sciences (Bible, dogmatics, church history, and practical theology). The shift, Farley notes, was not from piety to learning, but rather 'from one meaning of learning to another, from study which deepens heartfelt knowledge of divine things to scholarly knowledge of relatively discrete theological sciences' (p. 10). It was at this point that the fragmentation of theological education began. For it became increasingly unclear in the period from roughly 1850 to 1950 how the various sciences and disciplines represented in a typical theological faculty and curriculum are united by a common subject, namely *theology*.

The third period, according to Farley, emerged in the second half of this century. This new paradigm is predicted upon a view of 'the minister as professional' and 'recommends an education whose rationale lies in its power to prepare the student for designated tasks or activities which occur (or should occur) in the parish or in some specialised ministry.' On this model of education 'the theological student neither studies divinity nor obtains scholarly expertise in theological sciences, but trains for professional activities' (p. 11). Here theological education abandons the effort to find its unity in *theologia* and orients itself instead to the practice of ministry in one form or another.

Farley proposes that the issue of fragmentation can be resolved by reclaiming older and more adequate concepts of the nature of both theology and education. Education since the Enlightenment, he notes, has been understood increasingly as 'both learning and socialization in the discrete undertakings of scholarship'. Which is to say, 'Education means a communication of the many regions in which scholars and scientists divide up the cognitive universe' (p. 152). The typical undergraduate thus pursues a baccalaureate degree with a major in one of the natural sciences or the social sciences or the humanities. Lost from view is 'the ancient Greek ideal of culture (*paideia*), according to which education is the "culturing" of a human being in *arete* (virtue);' (p. 152-53). Substituting *theologia* (in the older sense of divinity) for *arete* (virtue), Farley contends for an ecclesial version of this Greek pedagogical ideal. Theology understood as divinity is conceived here as a form of existential wisdom or understanding, 'a sapiential knowledge engendered by grace and divine disclosure' (p. 153). On these terms, theological education is unified by the goal, not of professional competence in the practice of some form of ministry, but of the cultured or wise believer (student).

Farley's analysis of the present situation in theological education is accurate in my judgment, and the issue he has raised will remain on the agenda of theological educators until it is resolved in the future. Already a number of published responses to the challenge have appeared,[8] but

[8]See Joseph C. Hough, Jr. and John B. Cobb, Jr., *Christian Identity and Theological Education* (Chico, California: Scholars Press, 1985), and Max L. Stackhouse, *Apologia: Contextualisation, Globalisation, and Mission in Theological Education* (Grand Rapids, Michigan: William B. Eerdmans, 1988).

there is to date nothing like a consensus. Farley's own proposed solution enjoys two major benefits. By defining theology as a form of believing understanding or wisdom, he (a) makes it possible for the laity to recognise their personal role and stake in theology, and (b) resolves the current student-felt tension between theological formation (academics) and spiritual formation (piety) by uniting them. But by locating theology in the subjective development of the believer, he begs the question of the objective reality (God) that is the source and ground of such wisdom. The traditional notion of theology is that it has to do with the knowledge of God that is given by the Word (*Logos*) of God (*Theos*) attested in the Bible (hence: theology). Because Farley remains deferential to the modern canons of knowledge, he is compelled to dismiss the traditional view on the ground that it is dependent upon what he elsewhere calls pejoratively 'the house of authority'.

If my perception of the changes occurring in our intellectual culture is accurate, however, the traditional understanding of what theology is will receive a new lease on life in the public arena. Further, the Christian belief that the world was created by the Word of God, the same Word that became flesh in Jesus the Christ, entails the insight that the various aspects of created reality (Farley's 'many regions in which scholars and scientists divide up the cognitive universe') are not alien to God's Word. Knowledge of God the Creator illuminates, therefore, our knowledge of the creation. Professor Roy A. Clouser employs this insight in his important volume *The Myth of Religious Neutrality*, which is subtitled *An Essay on the Hidden Role of Religious Belief in Theories*.[9] Clouser's point is that all theoretical thought is predicated upon beliefs that are ultimately religious in

[9]Roy A. Clouser, *The Myth of Religious Neutrality: An Essay on the Hidden Role of Religious Belief in Theories* (Notre Dame, Indianna: The University of Notre Dame Press, 1991).

nature. He demonstrates how and why this is so of theories in mathematics as well as physics and psychology.

The implications of this are enormous for a post-critical philosophy of the nature and conditions of human knowledge and thus also for discerning how theological education coheres in its proper subject matter, theology. If all theoretical thought is in fact based upon beliefs that are religious in nature, then the knowledge of God given through the Church's 'foundational past' can and must serve as a critical intellectual tool in evaluating and using other theoretical and methodological disciplines that are useful for relating our knowledge of God to our knowledge of God's world, such as philosophy, psychology, sociology, and history. Theology as the knowledge of God grounded in the Word of God is, as Farley rightly insists, both existential and reflective. In its reflective mode, it informs the beliefs of theological students and enables them to deal both critically and profitably with other theoretical disciplines and methodologies represented in the faculties and curricula of our theological schools.

## IV

The identification of theology as an intellectual discipline and a pedagogical responsibility of discrete faith communities raises provocatively the issue of the place, if any, of theology in the educational milieu of the modern secular university. That this is an issue for the future of theological education is one of the ironies in the history of American higher education. For higher education had its origin on this continent in the vision of our colonial churches, a theologically informed vision of what is required of those who are called to love God with all of their minds as well as their hearts. Faith was initially the impetus for developing the life of the mind and pursuing knowledge in all fields, including the natural sciences. While it is inaccurate to claim, as some do, that such early colleges as Harvard, Yale and Princeton were founded for the primary purpose of training Christian ministers, it is true that these institutions served this purpose because the sponsoring churches (a) expected their clergy to be broadly educated and (b) believed that theology dealt with the subject matter (God) that integrated all fields of intellectual inquiry. Others have recounted the history and identified the causes of the displacement of this founding vision and its eventual replacement by another informed by the modern understanding of the nature and conditions of authentic knowledge.[10] Suffice it to say that the growing hegemony of the latter vision over the life of the university resulted not only in the dethroning of theology as the queen of the sciences but in its exile from the curriculum as well. Some institutions compensated theology by relegating it to their divinity schools which taught only students for the ministry. In other church-related colleges it found a home in the department of *religion*. But it was excluded from the great state universities that evolved after the Civil War ostensibly on the ground that the constitutional separation of church and state prohibited teaching sectarian doctrine in a state-funded institution. The actual reason, one suspects, is that theology had increasingly lost credibility as an authentic intellectual enterprise.

The issue remained virtually unchallenged until the student revolution of the 1960s. In the context of the intense social unrest of that period, occasioned but not caused by the Vietnam War, students rebelled against a system of higher education that venerated *objective* knowledge and claimed to be *value-free*. It was the Age of Aquarius, and the students challenged a curriculum that made no provisions for addressing basic issues of life, such as its meaning and values. Page Smith, the founding provost of the University of California at Santa Cruz, has written of the

---

[10]See Arthur J. De Jong, *Reclaiming a Mission: New Direction for the Church-Related College* (Grand Rapids, Michigan: William D. Eerdmans, 1990), pp. 3-82.

era that its cults demonstrated dramatically the basic human need not only for food and sex but equally 'the need to believe in something or somebody, a need expressed throughout history, most typically, by religion'.[11]

Whatever else the student revolt may have accomplished in changing higher education, it did result in the inauguration of serious religious studies programmes in many if not all colleges and universities. While the academic establishment granted the demand of students for courses in religion, it accommodated such instruction to its own intellectual standards of objective knowledge, free of value judgments regarding the truth of any particular religion or of religion itself. Religions are studied 'scientifically,' as phenomena that are subject to description but not evaluation. Religious studies has thus emerged as an independent humanistic discipline wed to the methods of the social sciences and the humanities. As such, it consciously distinguishes itself from theological studies and dissociates itself from communities of faith.

At the International Congress on Religion held in Melbourne in the summer of 1992, Dr Conrad Cherry gave an initial report on his research on the history of the relations between religious studies and theological education. He predicts a future of growing separation between the two academic enterprises. Cherry has found that religious studies faculty view theological studies as biased, because of its open faith commitments, and close-minded. Theological faculties conversely view religious studies as naive, because of its presumed objectivity, and irrelevant to believers. The issues are joined in the scholarly guilds, such as the American Academy of Religion and the Society of Biblical Literature, where religious studies faculty now form a numerical majority.

[11]Page Smith, *Killing the Spirit: Higher Education in America* (New York: Viking, 1990), p. 172.

How theological faculties individually and collectively come to terms with the intellectual standards and methodologies of the religious studies programme will influence decisively the direction of theological education in the future. The danger, as I see it, is that theologians will listen to the siren call of religious studies and adopt its understanding of the nature and conditions of human knowledge. Particularly vulnerable are the university-related divinity schools. According to Professor Cherry, the Divinity School of the University of Chicago has already shifted to a religious studies stance. Others may follow. If so, the pressure will be upon the so-called free-standing seminaries to follow suit. That would sound the death knell of theological education and probably of the churches that rely upon seminaries for their professional leadership.

My prediction is that the tides that currently move American intellectual culture are more favourable to theological education than to religious studies. Given the changes that are occurring in our understanding of what constitutes genuine knowledge, I do not see how the already outmoded model of knowledge inherited from the Enlightenment can continue for long to inform the ethos of the university. If theology will remain faithful to its own vision of knowledge that has its source in belief and is grounded in the truth mediated through tradition from the 'foundational past' of its faith community, it may anticipate a promising future and likewise, theological education, to the extent that it remains theological. The beneficiary will be the churches of the United States and, through them, the nation.

# 8

## TO SAVE THE EARTH
### CHARLES BIRCH

The future of our planet is in the balance. Sustainable development can be achieved, but only if irreversible degradation of the environment can be halted in time. The next 30 years may be crucial.

Joint statement by the Royal Society and the National Academy of Sciences. February 1992.

Because of the strain on resources it creates, materialism simply cannot survive the transition to a sustainable world.

Lester R. Brown (1990 p. 190)

Our generation has a litany of crimes against the world to its record. Top soil disappears at the rate of one football field each second. Arable land is covered with concrete at the rate of three football fields each minute. Forests disappear at the rate of four football fields each minute. Species disappear at the rate of 100 a day. Add to this the greenhouse effect and the hole in the ozone layer and it becomes obvious that our present treatment of the earth cannot continue forever.

We are on an unsustainable course. A flashing red light tells us that the scale and nature of human activity has grown out of proportion relative to the capacity of the earth to sustain it. Half the people in the world are poor, deprived, sick and dying of malnutrition and other preventable diseases. Our relations with other living creatures is that of a despot. We are fast destroying the environment on which all life depends. We have made our world an unhealthy place.

We need a change in consciousness to correctly diagnose the problems and a change in objective if we are to steer a safer course. That new objective can be stated quite simply. It is for an ecologically sustainable global society. This phrase was invented at a meeting of the World Council of Churches in 1974 as a response to the Club of Rome's report 'Limits to Growth' two years earlier. Its objective is for healthy (whole) people in a healthy environment, with healthy relations to that environment. The emphasis is on quality of life of the inhabitants of the earth for this and future generations.

In 1987 the report 'Our Common Future' of the World Commission on Environment and Development, also known as the Brundtland report, dropped the phrase ecologically sustainable society for 'sustainable development' (WCED 1987). That has turned out to be a mistake. It is vague enough that there are already over 80 definitions of sustainable development. Most of them as synonymous with sustained growth. Yet sustained growth is an impossibility for the world as a whole. Poor countries need economic growth. Rich countries need to curb their growth if we are to move toward an ecologically sustainable global society.

How can we hope to move from an unhealthy world to a healthy one? We need first to recognise the tremendous tension between technological progress and the health of the environment, including all organisms in it. Secondly, we need to recognise that tremendous tension between social injustice in the world and social justice. So destructive are these two tensions that many now wonder if what we call progress will eventually lead to our demise and that of the planet. The fundamental causes of environmental decline and poverty are inextricably linked. Jose Lutzenberger, Minister of Environment in Brazil, has said: 'If development is to be the continuation of the present mode and we must help developing countries to reach our level of affluence, while the developed countries must still continue developing to even higher levels of consumption, then what we are doing is suicidal' (Lutzenberger 1991, p. 11).

*The life-support systems of nature*
For millions of years the thin envelope of life around the earth, which we call the biosphere, has sustained the re-

sources necessary for life in a wonderful and complex way. We know only in part the complex relations involved. Some of them can be understood by considering what are called the life-support systems of nature.

A life-support system is analagous to the engineering system in a space vehicle that maintains an environment inside the vehicle to support the life of the cosmonaughts. They need an atmosphere to breathe, which means that the appropriate amount of oxygen and other gases has to be kept at a constant level, despite being constantly used up, while carbondioxide is constantly added from breathing. They have other requirements that have to be provided for such as appropriate temperature, air pressure and food, and wastes have to be disposed of as they are produced.

It is appropriate to regard the earth as a spaceship where the environment is maintained in such a way as to sustain life. Much of the science of ecology is concerned with finding out how this is done. Until recently we did not have to bother about this problem. The earth looked after itself. But as the number of human inhabitants increased and their activities became industrialised, we found we were disturbing the ecology of the planet in disastrous ways. The life-support systems were being threatened. To take one example. Carbondioxide is taken from the atmosphere by plants to make their plant tissues. It is returned to the atmosphere in the decomposition of plants and animals and in their breathing. Some of the carbondioxide in the atmosphere is absorbed by water in oceans and rivers. Not all animals and plants that die are decomposed immediately. Some of them have in the past been converted into coal and oil. When we burn fossil fuels, or for that matter the trees in forests, carbondioxide is returned to the atmosphere.

The balance between what is taken out of the atmosphere and what is returned has been remarkably constant over the ages. This is known from geological records. Since 1958, when measurements of carbondioxide in the atmosphere

were first made, the carbondioxide content of the atmosphere has been increasing. The combustion of fossil fuel
now augments the atmospheric carbondioxide by 0.7%
each year. A doubling of the concentration of this gas over
the pre-industrial level, at present rate of emissions, could
occur by the middle of the next century. If that happens the
earth's average temperature may rise between 1.5 and
4.5°C. Such a change could have profound and disastrous
effects on the climate of the world and the level of the
oceans. Much of Bangladesh, for example, could be inun-
dated.

The scientific evidence now indicates that global emissions of carbondioxide from the use of fossil fuels must be
reduced by 75% as soon as possible if over-heating of the
earth is to be avoided. Since the developed countries
produce about 75% of the carbondioxide that is added to
the atmosphere from fossil fuels, it is incumbent on them to
change their ways of getting energy. In the meantime the
industrial economy will have to be reduced drastically. As
the developing world becomes industrialised it will be
necessary for them, with the help of the developed work, to
find alternative sources of energy to fossil fuels. These are
enormously difficult problems that call for a global research effort.

A second example of the effect of humans on the life-
support systems of nature is on the food-cycle. Few people
seem to realise that all the resources used by humans, with
the exception of minerals and petroleum are dependent
upon four ecological systems: grasslands, croplands, forests
and fisheries. Yet each of these ecological systems is threatened; top soil is being lost at an alarming rate, forests are
being destroyed faster than they are renewed and fisheries
are overfished. All animal life including human life is
dependent upon plants. Animals either eat plants or they
eat animals that have eaten plants. Humans are now using
a disproportionate amount of the plant materials produced
on earth each year. Of all the plant material produced on

land each year humans use 40%. This has been a frightening figure for ecologists. The critical question becomes — how big can the human economy be, relative to the total ecosystem? Two more doublings of the economy sees us using over 100% of the world's ecological production! Yet the Brundtland report (WCED 1987) recommends an increase of five to ten times in the world economy if the poor nations are to lift their standard of living. This now seems to be ecologically impossible.

A working paper by economists of the World Bank (Goodland, Daly and El Serafy 1991), which includes two Nobel prize economists amongst the authors, finds that the Brundtland growth plan fails because it argues for a lifting of the bottom (the poor) rather than a lowering of the top (the rich) as well. The poor cannot be lifted unless the top falls. The rich must live more simply than the poor may simply live. That seems unacceptable to the rich world which considers that its own difficulties, such as inflation and unemployment, can only be remedied by increasing economic growth.

The world's cake of limited size will have to be carved up more equitably if the poor are to develop. More growth for the poor must be balanced by less growth for the rich. The present flow of wealth is greater from the poor world to the rich world. That will have to be reversed. Further the rich world, is responsible for most of today's environmental damage. It must therefore take the lead in changing direction. How can that happen?

Both the World Bank document and the 1991 report from the Club of Rome (King and Schneider 1991) argue that only a change in heart in the rich world will suffice. Economic rationalism must fly out the window to let ecological realism in. The consequence would be a drop in living standards of the rich world, although an increase in their quality of life. For example, to stop the contribution of the Netherlands to acidification of forests and lakes the Dutch would have to reduce the number of motorcar kilometres and farm livestock by half. The quality of the rain would be better but the standard of living would be lower.

*The environmental impact of humans*
Instead of thinking of the environmental impact of humans as a long list of components, we get a much better picture from a synoptic approach. By far the best proposal is that of Ehrlich, Ehrlich and Holdren (1977 p. 720) which was used as a basis for their later book on the population explosion (Ehrlich and Ehrlich 1990 p. 58). The impact of humans on the environment is viewed as a product of three components: (i) the number of people; (ii) a measure of the average person's consumption of resources (which is also an index of affluence) and (iii) an index of environmental disruptiveness of the technologies that provide the goods consumed. This component can also be viewed as the environmental impact per quantity of consumption. Hence:

$$\text{Impact} = \text{Population} \times \text{Affluence} \times \text{Technology}$$
$$\text{or}$$
$$I = PAT$$

Each of these components can in principle be measured, for example, resource use could be measured in terms of units of energy used per person. The T factor is difficult to measure as yet, but one index might be the grammes of sulphur dioxide produced per kilowatt hour of electricity generated. Much scientific research is called for to find ways of measuring T.

The equation shows that the components are multiplicative in their effect. Suppose that population, and the consumption of some commodity and the impact of technology per unit of consumption each increased threefold. The total impact increases 27-fold. The contributing components in this example are equally important, but each seems quite small compared to the total. Slowly growing components, when they multiply each other, lead to rapidly growing totals. Suppose we want to know whether population growth or rising consumption per person played the greater role in the growth of total energy consumption in the United States between 1880 and 1966. In this period, total energy consumption increased twelvefold while population increased fourfold. It may appear that consumption per person was a more important component than population growth. It was not. Consumption per person increased threefold, versus fourfold increase in the population. The twelvefold increase in the consumption of energy arose as the product, not the sum, of the fourfold increase in population and the threefold increase in consumption.

In poor countries P is large and A and T are small. In rich countries A and T are large and P is smaller. The total environmental impact can be reduced by reducing one or more of these components. In the case of the attack on the ozone layer by chlorofluorocarbons, the impact could be made negligible by operating on the T factor alone i.e. banning the offending chemical. This might result in a slight decrease in affluence if substitutes were more expensive. On the other hand, the injection of the major greenhouse gases, carbondioxide and methane, into the atmosphere is not so easily corrected.

The concentration of greenhouse gases in the atmosphere is tightly tied to the size of the population. Small per person changes can have enormous effects when multiplied by enormous numbers of people. There is probably no practical way to achieve the necessary reduction in greenhouse emissions without population control. Ehrlich and Ehrlich (1990 p. 113) have calculated an interesting example that illustrates this principle.

Suppose the United States decided to cut its contribution to the carbondioxide emissions by terminating all burning of coal. Suppose also that China's population remained at 1.1 billion. Suppose secondly that China scaled back its development plans so that it only doubled its per person consumption of coal. That would raise China's per person use of energy to some 14 per cent of that in the United States. This modest advance in development in China with its huge population would more than offset the reduction of carbondioxide emissions achieved by the total abandonment of coal by the United States.

## Population

Population is the P factor in the PAT equation of environmental impact. Population is always a component of environmental impact. People who think that population is no longer important point to the growth of population in Western countries which has slowed, with zero growth in 13 countries. And some Asian countries have managed to reduce their rate of population growth in recent years.

What these people fail to appreciate is that despite this, the annual global increase in population in 1991 was an all time high reaching nearly 100 million more people being added to the planet. The fact remains that the 1990s will see the greatest increase in human numbers of any decade in history. If by some way humanity were able to reduce the environmental impact of all its technologies by 10% and there were no increase in personal affluence, world population increase would return the collective impact of humans to the previous level in about five years. Just about every step forward in the A and T items of the PAT equation are negated by population growth.

The world's population in 1991 was estimated to be 5.4 billion. It is likely to reach 6.3 billion by the end of this century, nearly the equivalent of adding another China. More than 90 per cent of the increase in poor countries. That poses an immense problem for the rich world and the poor world alike.

If every woman in the world from this year had no more than 2.2 surviving children, which is replacement reproduction, the world's population would still grow. This is because population growth has a momentum such that it takes about two generations before curbs applied now have a major effect. Some European countries have expressed a concern at having reached replacement reproduction. Yet these same countries cannot avoid a 20% or 30% increase in numbers, even if they maintain replacement reproduction. To achieve zero population growth in the 20th century, even in the most developed countries, birth-rates would have to fall well below replacement levels. This seems unlikely. If replacement reproduction for the developed world as a whole had begun in the 1980s the population would still increase by more than a quarter, adding some 300 million more people.

For these reasons it is important to reduce birth-rates as soon as possible. A reduction in the birth-rate now takes many years to be reflected in numbers of people. The concept of population momentum may be a difficult ecological concept to grasp, but it is not difficult to understand its effects. That understanding should be far more widespread than it is. Precisely because population growth is slow to be controlled, it is the issue to tackle now.

Many ecologists believe that the world is now overpopulated. The environment cannot stand the further pressure which more people is putting upon it. Overpopulation is deleterious because:

* it reduces the chance that all the people in the world can be adequately fed and housed. The increase in food production in the world following the Green Revolution has hardly done more than maintain the existing amount of food per person, because of the continuous increase in population

* it increases the pressure on most other resources, many of which are difficult to obtain

* it accentuates the problem of urbanisation. Increased population means more people migrate to already overcrowded cities such as Sao Paulo and Calcutta

* it negates the effect of economic development in poor countries and in rich countries exaggerates still further their disproportionate consumption of the world's resources

and their disproportionate contribution to pollution.

The 1990s is now regarded as the crucial decade which will determine population trends over the next century. Immediate action is required on a number of fronts. Rapid population growth is now widely recognised as a hindrance to development in poor countries. In the 1970s there was a widespread notion that 'development is the best contraceptive'. We now know that this is an over-simplification. Such traditional measures of development as GNP per person and urbanisation seem to have little or no relation to birth-rates and therefore population growth.

On the other hand, certain kinds of development do foster reduction in the birth-rate. 'Social development' as opposed to 'economic development' seems to hold the key here. For example, adequate nutrition is important. Some people in the past have argued that the more food the poor get the larger will be their families, that extra food is converted into extra babies. The fact is that denying people food does not lower their birth-rates. It increases death-rates.

Providing adequate food in conjunction with improvement in socio-economic conditions lowers the birth-rate. Improvement in socio-economic conditions that motivate parents to have fewer children include: parental confidence about the future, improved status for women, literacy, better health and sanitation. All these measures lead to a sense of greater security and are effective in lowering birth-rates. Increased economic equality greatly accelerates the process, as does land reform. It is not necessary that per person GNP be very high, certainly not as high as that of the rich countries during their gradual demographic transition from high rates of growth to low rates. In other words, lower birth-rates in poor countries can be achieved long before the conditions exist that were present in the rich countries in the late 19th and early 20th centuries. At the same time as socio-economic conditions are improved, vigorous family planning programmes become effective when they were ineffective before these measures were taken.

At least 13 countries have managed to reduce their birth-rates by an average of more than one birth per thousand population per year for periods of five to 16 years. Such a reduction would bring birth-rates in poor countries to replacement level by the turn of the century. These countries include Taiwan, Singapore, Costa Rica, South Korea, Egypt, Chile, China, Cuba and Sri Lanka. To stop population growth world-wide, birth-control would have to grow from about 50 to 70 per cent of couples, and average family size would have to decrease from about four to two children.

*Affluence: the consumption of resources*
This is the A factor in the PAT equation. As already mentioned it is little appreciated that four biological systems, croplands, forests, grasslands and fisheries, provide all the resources for the economy except for fossil fuels, minerals and water. Croplands supply food, fibre, vegetable oils and such like. Grasslands provide meat, milk, leather and wool. Forests provide timber, lumber and paper.

The share of the land planted to crops increased from the time agriculture began until 1981. Since then the area of newly reclaimed land has been offset by that lost to degradation and conversion to non-farm use. The area of grassland has shrunk since the mid-seventies, as overgrazing converts it into desert. Forests have shrunk for centuries, but the losses accelerated in the middle of this century and even more from 1980 onwards. The combined area of the three biologically productive systems on land is shrinking, while what is left, wasteland and areas covered with human settlements, are expanding.

Until world population reached three billion in 1960 the yields of the five biological systems, croplands, grasslands, fisheries and forests expanded more rapidly than population. By the time the population had reached four billion in 1976 the per-person production of forest wood, the products of grasslands; beef, mutton and wool, began to decline and have continued that trend ever since. The fish catch had been growing at a record rate for two decades prior to 1970, but since 1970 the fish catch per person fell by 13 per cent or over one per cent per year. Then 15 years later in the mid 1980s there was an upturn of nearly 20% due largely to the recovery of one single fishery, the over-fished Peruvian anchoveta fishery.

Turning from per-person production to total global production, the total production from forests has been declining for several years. There was an enormous growth in grain production from croplands between 1950 and 1984. But it fell sharply in 1987 and that fall has continued. Per-person grain production varied from region to region. During the 1950s and 1960s, grain production exceeded population growth on every continent, diets improved almost everywhere. Beginning in the 1970s, however, production in Africa fell behind population growth, leading to a fall in production per person of about one tenth. During the 1980s, Africa has been joined by Latin America, whose decline dates from 1982, the year the debt crisis began. In Japan, Taiwan and South Korea, production of grain has been declining since 1967. Japan's historically excellent, productive and sustainable agricultural system is being destroyed by deforestation, development, pollution and pesticides. From a peak production in 1967 Japan's production of grain fell by more than one quarter in ten years.

It is pretty clear that human demand is now outstripping the sustainable yield of the natural biological systems that support the world economy. The concept of sustainable yield is an ecological one. It refers to the yield that can be sustained without causing deterioration of the carrying capacity of the resource and therefore a reduction in yield. For example, intensive studies of the effect of fish-catch on yield led to the conclusion in the early seventies that the total global fish catch could be sustained at about 100 million tonnes a year. If more than that were fished the yield would not be sustained. It seems now that prediction was too optimistic.

The deterioration of soil on agricultural lands is world wide. The world as a whole loses top soil equivalent to the top soil of the entire huge wheat belt of Australia each year. The United States is in the midst of a programme to convert at least 16 million hectares of eroded cropland, 11% of the total, to grassland or woodland before it loses more. Much agriculture in the United States, as in Australia, is unsustainable, that is to say present practices are causing soil deterioration with reduction in crop yields. The causes are manifold, including overuse of chemical fertilisers that tend to destroy soil structure, salting from irrigation and water and wind erosion.

Deserts are expanding as a result of inappropriate land use in Africa, south-central Asia, Australia, the Western United States and southern South America. In China between 1949, when the Communist government came into power, and the year 2000 it is estimated that the total area of desert will have doubled.

The deterioration of natural productive systems in the many ways so far discussed exemplifies an ecological principle that over-use converts renewable resources into non-renewable ones. It uses them faster than they can be renewed. When this happens soil becomes unsustainable for cropping and forests do not regenerate. Another example of this principle is the extent to which water is being taken out of underground stores (aquifiers) many times faster than it is being replaced by nature. This is happening to the acquifier underlying the Great Plains of the United States, the Artesian Basin of Central Australia and possible also the great underground stores of water in the Sahara desert, fed from the Atlas Sahasrile mountains in north west Algeria. Oil industries in the desert are drawing enormous quantities of water from this aquifier. Likewise the rate of withdrawal of water from the Colorado river is now about equal to its flow.

A major biological resource that is being drastically depleted as a consequence of human activity is the diversity of life of micro-organisms, plants and animals. This depletion of species is referred to as the reduction of biodiversity. We do not know how many species there are, possibly over 30 million. We do know that the tropics provide the richest array of plants, insects, birds and mammals. More than a third of all known species of flowering plants are native to tropical America. Tropical rain forests that cover just 7% of the earth's land surface may contain more than 40% of all living species of plants and animals. Yet it is these forests that are being destroyed faster than any other.

A single hectare of Peruvian rainforest has 41,000 species of insects in the forest canopy. One isolated ridge-top in the Andean foothills of western Ecuador only 20 square kilo-metres in area, lost as many as 90 unique plant species when the last of its forest was cleared to make way to plant subsistance crops.

We do not know which are all the critical species involved in the life-support systems of the planet, nor those that might be useful in the future for creating new crops and new medicines. To answer that question requires a huge research effort in ecology that is hardly as yet being tackled. A probable estimate of species lost is that about 100 species are becoming extinct each day. This is a tremendous loss in the diversity of life on this planet. Most of the loss is due to the destruction of habitats such as forests, especially those in the tropics. The rate of tropical deforestation in 1989 was double that in 1979 with about 1.8% of the remaining forests disappearing each year.

Agriculture has been greatly dependent upon wild varieties for genes that increase productivity, give resistance to disease and enable varieties to be produced that can withstand drought, cold and other extremes of weather. The wild relatives of commercial varieties, ranging from tomatoes to wheat, have provided genes worth billions of dollars in higher crop yields.

Recognition of this has earned these wild relatives the label 'the newest resource'. They become increasingly important as advances in biotechnology make possible the transfer of genes, not just from one variety to another, but from one species to another. Genes of known existing varieties are now being preserved in 'gene banks' set up in 13 international centres. The idea is also being explored of establishing 'gene parks' where crop-species can be kept under cultivation. In addition to the preservation of wild strains of crop plants there is the possibility of discovering altogether new crops. Only a few of the more than a quarter of a million kinds of plants that exist have been investigated for this purpose. Much remains to be done before we make too many more species extinct.

What can be done about the loss in biodiversity? Since most of the loss is species is a result of destruction of habitats it is clear that prevention of further losses means that this sort of activity has to be severely restricted. Instead, reserves for the preservation of habitats need be created such as the 252 reserves established in 66 countries under UNESCO's Biosphere programme. Acts of parliament need to be passed, as in the state of Victoria in Australia, to provide for the preservation of endangered species by preserving critical habitats.

In addition to habitat destruction, the disappearance of species is associated with other forms of deterioration of the environment. There is evidence that species of frogs are becoming rarer throughout the world. Many of these declines are occurring in the absence of destruction of habitats, suggesting other causes such as pollution from pesticides, acid rain and increases in ultraviolet exposure or other changes in climate.

An indispensable strategy for saving our fellow living creatures is to diminish the scale of human activities. Both the size of the human population and the environmental impact of the average individual must eventually be reduced well below what it is today. Unless we can move in that direction all other efforts will be for naught. Basic to any of these activities is a change in consciousness about our other living inhabitants of the earth. Instead of simply valuing other species in terms of their usefulness to us, we need to respect them for their intrinsic value. That is to say we need to recognise that they too have feelings of pain and pleasure and their lives are of value to themselves and to God as our lives are of value to each of us and to God. They too have a right to live. But I know of only one government in the world which includes the words 'intrinsic value' of other creatures in its legislation. That is the government of New Zealand. Would that others made that recognition.

In addition to biological resources, the life of humans is dependent upon non-renewable resources, notably fossil fuels and minerals. These are appropriately discussed in the next section on the impact of technology on environment.

*Technology: its environmental impact*
The environmental disruptiveness of technologies used to produce the goods consumed by society is the T factor in the PAT equation. They include the production of toxic substances, both from the normal operation of industry such as ionizing radiation and carbondioxide and from disasters such as the Chernobyl nuclear explosion, and certain products of industry such as pesticides, and chlorofluorocarbons. By far the most important source of disruption of the environment comes from the use of fossil fuels for energy. Coal was the main offender after the Industrial Revolution began. In the middle of the 19th century coal began to be displaced by oil and later oil has been complemented by natural gas.

Ours is essentially a petroleum culture. But it is not the exhaustion of fossil fuels that is the primary concern. It now seems certain that we shall have to phase out the use of these sources of energy well before the reserves are gone. Indeed it could be said in general, that since the Club of Rome's 1972 report 'Limits to Growth' the constraints have shifted from resource limits to what are called 'sink limits', that is the use of the planet as a sink for our wastes. How much more can the biosphere stand?

What can be done about this? There are two components in the move to a more ecologically sustainable society concerning use of energy. One is a shift to renewable resources of energy such as solar energy and wind. The other is increase in efficiency in the use of energy. The latter is the one that is more easily dealt with. Between 1973 and 1984 energy efficiency in the United States rose by 23% despite economic growth. This saved ten million barrels of oil a day. Western Europe, starting with substantially more efficient economies, realised a 16% increase in efficient use of energy over the same period. Japan did even better. On the other hand Greece and Australia were less efficient during this period. Simple steps such as better insulation and more efficient heating and cooling systems in houses are effective ways to conserve energy. Even quite small changes in technology can have dramatic effects in reducing environmental impact. In the United States the Reagan administration relaxed the efficiency standards of automobiles that had already been met by Chrysler. If these regulations had been kept in place, within a decade or so the amount of gasoline saved would have been equivalent to the entire amount of oil estimated to underlie the Arctic National Wildlife Refuge. That single step could have both removed a threat to one of the last really wild places on earth and it would have reduced air pollution in cities.

*Conclusion*
The world needs to be saved because it is moving in an ecologically unsustainable path. The global economy cannot continue growing indefinitely on a finite planet. Even a twofold increase is likely to be perilous for the biosphere.

The transition to an ecologically sustainable global society involves no less than a revolution. There is no precedent for the many changes needed. Building an ecologically sustainable future depends upon restructuring the global economy, major shifts in human reproductive behaviour to move to zero population growth, reduced consumption of goods in the rich world, improved standards of living in the poor world, an efficient recycling of materials, a move away from fossil fuels to the use of renewable sources of energy. There must be dramatic changes in human consciousness, in values and life-style from a materialistic style of life to one that emphasises instead quality of life.

Lester Brown, in the State of the World Report for 1992 says that if this revolution succeeds, it will rank with the Agricultural and Industrial Revolutions as one of the great transformations in human history (Brown 1992). The first two revolutions were driven by technological advances, the first by the discovery of farming and the second by the invention of the steam engine, which converted the energy of coal into mechanical power. The environmental revolution will also use new technologies but in an extraordinarily wide range of areas. While it will use new technologies, it will be driven, not primarily by technological advances, but by a new vision of an ecologically sustainable global economy that involves new values and new economic and social policies. The Agricultural Revolution began 10,000 years ago. The Industrial Revolution has been under way for two centuries. But if the environmental revolution is to succeed it must be compressed into a few decades. This is an enormous challenge to every inhabitant of the earth, to economists, sociologists, politicians, scientists technologists, and also to philosophers, clergy and theologians, that they might help to mobilise rethinking of our basic values and vision of progress.

## REFERENCES

Brown, Lester, R. (Ed.) 1990. *State of the World. 1990.* New York, W. W. Norton and Co.

Brown, Lester, R. 1992. Launching the environmental revolution, pp. 174-190. In Brown, Lester R. *State of the World.* 1992. New York, W. W. Norton and Co.

Ehrlich, Paul R. and Ehrlich, Anne H. 1990. *The popu-lation explosion.* New York, Simon and Schuster.

Ehrlich, Paul R. Ehrlich, Anne, H. and Holdren, John P. 1977. *Ecoscience: population, resources, environment.* San Francisco, Freeman and Co.

Goodland, Robert, Daly, Herman E. and Salah, El Serafy. 1991. Environmentally sustainable economic development: building on Brundtland. Washington. *Economic Working Paper No. 46 of the World Bank.*

Joint Statement by the Royal Society and the National Academy of Sciences 1992. *Population growth, resource consumption and a sustainable world.* Press Release 27 February 1992.

King, Alexander and Bertrand Schneider 1991. *The first global revolution.* New York, Simon and Schuster.

WCED. 1987. *Our common future.* Oxford University Press.

# 9

## THE CHALLENGE TO BUSINESS IN THE 1990s

### WILLIAM E. SIMON

The truly great man is that man who never reminds us of another.

So wrote Ralph Waldo Emerson in 1850. And, those words he penned are a perfect description of Sir John Templeton, a bold and brilliant investor whose heroic success on Wall Street is matched only by his generous spirit and giant heart — a quiet gentleman, who is truly one of God's noblemen.

John Templeton is, in every respect, a superior man.

For, while many in America profit from the economic freedoms of the enterprise system, and many defend the principles of that system, as well, rare are those who demonstrate through their personal example the discipline, thrift, wise judgment and untarnished integrity that lie at the heart of our system's strength and success.

John Templeton is that kind of man. He is the kind of man all of us aspire to be.

I have always believed that character shapes the destiny of individuals and of nations. So, it is fitting to begin these reflections on America's future, by pointing to the convictions of an individual who has reached the pinnacle of personal achievement.

John Templeton has been many things in his life — devoted family man, entrepreneur, community leader, philanthropist.

But, the guiding compass of all his beliefs and endeavours has been his abiding faith in God.

Faith is John Templeton's core. And his is a faith that sees spiritual growth developing in harmony with physical health and material prosperity. For John, there is no contradiction between spiritual and material fulfilment.

133

He believes that free enterprise is a tremendous force for human good, flowing from the heart of our Judeo-Christian beliefs and traditions.

And thus, he believes each of us is called to be creative in the image of our Creator. And, we are called to serve.

In his Gospel of Wealth, Andrew Carnegie wrote that the duty of the man of wealth is to set an example of modest, unostentatious living, shunning display or extravagance, to provide for the legitimate wants of those dependent upon him; and, after doing so, to consider surplus resources that come to him as trust funds to be administered for his poorer brethren, bringing to their service his wisdom and experience.

This is John Templeton!

John Templeton's whole life, from his academic accomplishments at Yale and as a Rhodes Scholar, to the stunning success of the Templeton Growth Fund and to the establishment of the Templeton Prize, reflect the strength of his conviction that faith and liberty are the linchpins of all human progress, and of his life-long commitment to our free enterprise system and the traditional values of our free society.

What a remarkable man! And, what a remarkable standard of leadership he sets, when we consider the constant drumbeat today, criticising the levels of executive compensation and the quest for golden parachutes, as well as corporate corruption and overall unethical behaviour.

John Templeton's convictions and success are a model for us all during these uncertain times when the American people feel besieged by problems and search for reasons to feel hopeful about our future.

Now, I am personally convinced we have good reason to feel hopeful. And, while I am, by nature, a prudent man, for the first time in my life, I am unabashedly optimistic about the future, and the potential of free people to create a prosperity beyond any we have ever known before.

In making that statement, I certainly do not want to dismiss the difficulties we face at home and across the globe.

In the United States, rising taxes, regulations and an explosion of debt have weakened our economy, creating a drag on global growth and raising the spectre of financial crisis.

The Federal government now consumes 25 per cent of the GNP, with the deficit approaching $400 billion and the national debt at nearly $4 trillion.

In the former Soviet Union, the struggling, young democracies and the desperate condition of their economies have threatened millions with starvation, and the continent of Europe with increasing instability.

And, across the world, the move toward regional trading blocs — with Europe 1992, Asian Rim economies under the leadership of Japan, and the North American Trading Zone — is intended to promote comparative advantage and economies of scale.

On the other hand, these blocs could also jeopardize trade flows and lock in more insular patterns of commerce.

These problems must be faced squarely by the leaders of the world's industrial nations. Yet, they should not blind us to a far greater force, a truly epic force bringing epic changes to people across the world.

In a word, that force is freedom. Freedom is winning — not all at once, to be sure, and, more often than not with steps that lurch and stagger.

Nevertheless, when the history of the last decade of the 20th century is written, I believe it will be remembered not for years of global recession and retrenchment, but for recovery and renewal.

And that progress will be thanks to our faith in a system of political, personal and economic liberties rooted in the principles of the God-given dignity of every individual, the rights of private property, and the opportunity to work within free markets to build a better future for our children and our children's children.

Everywhere we look — from Brazil to Berlin and even to the streets of Beijing — a great stirring has begun; and one can only be struck by the quickening pace of change, and, by the remarkable victory of the ideas of capitalism.

Across the world, capitalism, with entrepreneurs responding to consumers in free markets, is moving forward, while socialism, communism and every other form of 'ism', where citizens must conform to the diktats of politicians and bureaucrats, is in retreat.

These watershed events were given tremendous impetus by the leadership of President Reagan, when he fundamentally redirected America's economic policies toward growth and opportunity.

And, others did not hesitate to pick up that banner.

Industrious and inventive people in the Far East have been building a giant economic superpower among the nations of the Pacific Rim.

Latin American countries which, for generations, shunned the free market, are today in the vanguard of the movement to limit government, lower tax rates, deregulate and privatise their industries, create sound currencies and open their markets.

We are even beginning to see the outlines of a solution to the Latin American debt crisis. Recognition is finally dawning in that region that bailouts without structural reform amount to little more than throwing good money after bad.

And, the collapse of the Soviet Empire portends the coming of a radically new political and economic order before the dawn of the 21st century.

America's place is surely not to sit back and let others pioneer this exciting future. Our challenge, and in particular, the challenge to the Business Community, is to harness these historic forces for change — to unleash the dynamics of human liberty to move America and the whole world closer to the triumph of freedom and a Golden Age of democratic capitalism.

As Fortune Magazine noted, if a new world is, indeed, to be born in the aftermath of the Cold War, the midwife will be business leadership. For, just as the power of the nation-state eclipsed the church following the Reformation of the

16th century, so now the corporation is beginning to over-take the state.

We see the proof in the growth of global markets, with the proliferation of split-second, communication technolo-gies, international joint ventures and strategic alliances, as well as the rash of privatisation sweeping across companies, countries and continents.

All are signs of the growing importance of corporations competing on the new, global playing field, where borders are fading, distance has become trivial, and labour and capital have become highly mobile as firms seek their best use.

My good friend and colleague, former U.S. Secretary of State, George Shultz, illustrated these changes when he spoke of a shipping label on integrated circuits which read:

'Made in one or more of the following countries: Korea, Hong Kong, Malaysia, Singapore, Taiwan, Mauritius, Thai-land, Indonesia, Mexico, Philippines — the exact country of origin is unknown.'

So, given the rising influence and importance of busi-ness, let me turn to the responsibility of American business leaders — to help create an Agenda for the Future, for American enterprise, for our country and for the world.

That agenda must begin with the inescapable reality of our time. Today's Chief Executives live and work in a global marketplace.

Increasingly, they find themselves having to compete with companies in Frankfurt, Seoul and Singapore for capital, projects and markets.

Thus, they must be prepared to think, plan and act in new ways, taking a more global view of joint venturing, capital formation and locating new plants.

And, in this age of global markets, it is useful to remind ourselves, as I know John Templeton would, what markets reward most. And, the clear answer is that markets reward value, which, itself, is a product of smart investments and innovation, and of superior quality and timing.

Or, as author Alvin Toffler puts it, survival of the fittest in the 90s will mean survival of the fastest and the smartest.

We will have to be faster and smarter to stay one step ahead of the power curve. We will have to know the relative strengths and weaknesses of the economies in which we participate.

We will have to know how to customize products and services; and we will have to be nimble enough to enter alliances to share the financial risk of sponsoring vital research and developing new technologies that can help increase market access and strengthen market share.

And, we will have to know how to capitalise one speed — speed in making transactions, creating new ideas and bringing those ideas to market.

In sum, we will have to think globally and act locally.

And, I believe that we are doing all of these things better than we did before. I say this with full knowledge of the harsh criticisms that have been levelled against American corporations and workers.

Granted, for too long, we read too many press clippings and all but lulled ourselves to sleep with the illusion that America's industrial predominance was an economic given that would endure forever.

Nevertheless, I am a strong believer that we need to encourage each other, remember our natural entrepreneurial strengths, gain confidence from our achievements and, above all, not tear America down.

Because, while we are being severely tested and challenged, the truth is, we have not been overwhelmed, we are fighting back and our exports are rising, not falling.

Today, we are seeing a far more competitive and aggressive American presence in the global marketplace. My own business dealings have taken me increasingly to the Far East, and I've been struck to see that there are now over 800 American firms located in Hong Kong.

And, many of them are small, innovative, young growth companies who are nipping at the heels of the traditional industry giants and grabbing their market share.

But, in recent years, America's largest corporations have also responded to the global challenge through vigilant efforts to cut costs, accept lay-offs and make the painful adjustments to upgrade productivity and manufacture products of superior quality.

For example, since 1986, the American automobile industry has dramatically upgraded the quality of U.S. cars, exceeding the rate of improvement of Japanese autos. And, despite its problems at home, General Motors has done exceptionally well in Europe, even managing to gain a bigger share of the East German market than Volkswagen.

U.S. steelmakers have utilised joint ventures to gain an infusion of capital and new technology to improve their manufacturing processes. Result? They have cut in half the time needed to produce a metric ton of steel and they are now out-producing the Japanese.

Indeed, for all the talk of America's decline, we still produce a quarter of the world's GNP, and we lead the world in key industries from aeronautics to biotechnology, data processing, entertainment, health care, pharmaceuticals, software, speciallty chemicals, supercomputer and telecommunications, to cite a few.

We are regaining our speed and our strength. But, we cannot afford to slacken our pace, for the business community is clearly the leading catalyst for peaceful change and greater prosperity, both in America and the world.

The more innovative, agile and successful business can be, the stronger we can be as that vital engine of growth that strengthens America and the global economy, and helps lead the nations of Eastern Europe and the Third World on to the road of democratic capitalism.

In the 1930s, Winston Churchill said, 'I was not the lion, but it fell to me to give the lion's roar.' Well, today, it falls to the leaders of the business community to give the lion's roar for freedom.

To believe is to be strong, and to lead. And, business must

lead in the 90s as a defender and a champion of free and open markets, and as a competitor ready to seize opportunities now blossoming across the globe.

In the former Soviet Union and Eastern Europe, the business community should be on the front lines of the struggle to create radically new economies centred around private companies, private payrolls and private enterprise.

I believe that Boris Yeltsin is a strong, principled, courageous man, and a friend of the West. But, his problems are monumental and he needs our help. And, providing help is not only politically and economically sound, but also morally right.

For, the struggle to feed, clothe and house those people, and to privatize, marketize and monetize those economies is so great, and the consequences of failure so potentially grave, that the sooner we can help those people cross their threshold of danger, the better it will be for all the world.

Already, the celebration and euphoria have given way to the harsh reality that freedom is not free.

With shattered economies, high inflation, and precious, little working knowledge of free markets, the people have seen prices soar, distribution systems buckle and millions of jobs disappear as the doors of inefficient enterprises have been slammed shut.

The people of Eastern Europe have discovered that the price of freedom if high, indeed, very high.

Will they have the patience and will their new governments prove sufficiently strong and stable to withstand these shocks and dislocations?

We do not know, but the odds will improve if people feel they're being given not warmed-over socialism, but opportunities to take charge of their lives and rebuild their countries.

That is why I agree with those who urge us not to repeat the mistakes the West has made for decades, by inundating countries with loans and government planners. Instead, we should help them clear away the clutter of regulations, high tax rates and state-directed development plans that shackle their aspiring entrepreneurs.

Eastern Europe does not need a new Marshall Plan, it needs a free-market plan that helps it marshal opportunity.

Czechoslovakia's wonderful President, Vaclav Havel, put it so well when he addressed our Congress and pleaded with America — do not send us your wealth, send us your knowledge, so we can learn to create wealth.

This is what business must do, not only by lending our voices to support property rights, free markets and sound currencies, but also our direct support — through our human, intellectual and investment capital — to help these countries transfer ownership and control of public lands, farms and factories to managers, workers and stockholders.

Progress will not come overnight. But providing our assistance company-to-company, project-by-project, people-to-people, is the best way to ensure that progress will come, and that it will last.

As developing countries from Eastern Europe to Latin America push forward on domestic reforms, their success and eventual ability to pay down their large loans could rest on their access to equitable commercial ties and trading relationships.

And, that access is not a given. Consider the example of Europe 1992. The dismantling of economic barriers in the European Community, and the rewarding of countries according to their comparative advantage could harness the economic potential of 350 million people with a GNP of nearly $5 trillion.

Freed of remaining constraints, Western Europe could become a new economic powerhouse.

However, should the authorities in Brussels simply replace regulations in individual countries with new community-wide regulations, and restrict their open-market policies to European members only, then Europe 1992 may not turn out to be a great, liberating force for the future, but a bureaucratic fortress that encroaches upon enterprise and stifles economic freedom and entrepreneurship.

And, we have seen disturbing signs. European agricultural policies remain rigidly protectionist. And, while Eastern European countries have eagerly opened their economies to Western European investments, the goods they manufacture for export are often shut out of Western European markets.

In times of global stress, when moods turn somber and the outlook seems most grim, demand for protectionist polices invariably grows louder.

We have heard these same demands in our own country. But, the lessons of history are clear, and no credible economist, left or right, believes that protectionism and beggar-thy-neighbour policies will bring anything but havoc and misery to the economies and lives of people everywhere.

We are the leaders of the free world. Alexander Solzehenitsyn warned that if the United States does not lead, the free world will have no leader.

Our responsibilities are not easy, but an America with its head buried in the sand today, will mean a world where freedom is buried tomorrow. A 'Fortress America' mentality will only fortify those who oppose freedom, and we all know there are many such despots waiting in the wings.

We should support an 'America First' policy, as long as it's America first in leading the world, not retreating from it.

Obviously, the world is a messy place, filled with trade tensions and inequities which must be addressed. But, our goal must remain free markets, for, simply put, the freer each individual, and the freer each individual market, the more people can prosper and businesses can flourish.

And, the battle for free markets should not be left to the politicians alone. Business has a vested interest, and we need the leadership of companies like IBM and Archer Daniels to help mount a global drive to open markets in Europe and the Americas, as well as the dynamic markets of the Pacific to achieve higher levels of world commerce and trade.

Because, at a time when trade negotiations have repeatedly hit the wall of European intransigence, and when Japan should be renouncing protectionist policies and opening its markets to a much greater extent than it does — there is a clear opening for American initiative, ingenuity and audacity.

We have in place a US-Canadian free trade agreement — and it is successful.

We are putting in place a similar agreement with Mexico, which has already created an estimated 350,000 jobs, as well as with other countries of the Americas.

So, why not go further? We now have an opportunity to establish free-trade agreements with the members of the former Soviet Bloc.

And, a Western Hemispheric free trade zone, stretching from Point Barrow, Alaska, to Cape Horn at the southern tip of South America, combining with a US free trade zone with the nations of Southeast Asia and the Pacific Rim, would include over one billion people.

Our combined GNP would dwarf the European Economic Community. So, I believe that the greatest bulwark against protectionism in one part of the world, is dynamic, expanding economies in other parts of the world.

Our message should be, let us help each other and trade together. Let us lower barriers and wipe out tariffs together, and we will create a prosperity so powerful that, to borrow the words of former President Reagan, we will not just defeat our competition, we will transcend it.

And, we should move now, in this pivotal moment while the time is still ripe — while the new democracies in Eastern Europe are sorting out, while the European Economic Community is still coming together, and the Japanese face the challenges in their own changing culture.

As Shakespeare wrote in Julius Caesar, 'There is a tide in the affairs of men, Which, taken at the flood, leads on to fortune; Omitted, all the voyage of their life Is bound in shallows and miseries.'

Let us not delay, nor forget that the success of our efforts across the world will ultimately hinge on the success of our efforts at home — to build a productive and powerful economy capable of delivering sustained, non-inflationary growth.

And, certainly, it is valid to ask, how can we expect to win the battle for global markets, when we have failed to take responsibility for our own system at home?

The sad spectacle of chronic budget deficits, 34 in the last 35 years, of our Savings and Loan industry in distress, of long-term interest rates remaining abnormally high, and of a public education system awarding diplomas to a shamefully, unskilled workforce — is vivid proof that we have accepted, with ever less reluctance and embarrassment, actions and practices plainly inconsistent with the principles of responsible freedom we inherited from generations preceding us.

The proper responsibility of government is not to control our lives, but to create conditions for our economy to grow in a non-inflationary environment — for jobs to be created, businesses to expand and people to be encouraged to save and invest for their future and for their children's future.

This is freedom's way.

But, our government has far exceeded that mandate. It has created programmes we cannot afford based on revenues that are not there. It has put more and more of what was on-budget, off-budget, and done all of this with fiscal sleight-of-hand that has contaminated the entire budget process and weakened the financial moorings of this country.

Certainly, these problems did not appear overnight. Governmental excesses began to take root in the late 1960s, when our leaders were telling America we could afford guns and butter, even as their boom-bust policies were laying the seeds for an inflationary nightmare.

I served in Washington in the 1970s and saw, first-hand, the frightful consequences of those economic mistakes. I watched us lurch from inflation to recession and back to inflation; from currency devaluations, to closing the gold window; from price controls to the energy crisis; and all of this culminating in Watergate, which nearly tore our country apart.

In the 1980s, President Reagan's programme to reduce high tax-rates and the mountains of paperwork and regulations revived our entrepreneurial spirit. And, passage of the Gramm-Rudman legislation, mandating steadily, declining deficits even began to slow, although not reverse, the persistent trend of government spending growing faster than the underlying economy.

Unfortunately, the imposition of new tax burdens in 1990, and a host of new regulations on business have left us mired in slow growth, rising budget deficits, with individuals, corporations and governments all financially stretched.

Moreover, as our economy has languished, Washington has all but lost itself in political demagoguery.

To cite one example, investment capital is the lifeblood of the free enterprise system — the centrepiece of risk-taking and investment in the free enterprise system is its capital-raising system. Yet, in the United States, the presumed, free-market leader of the world, we tax capital gains at a higher rate than virtually any other developed country.

As Fortune magazine recently noted, 'An adventurous startup that doubled in value over the past decade would provide its investors with a return, after inflation and capital gains tax, of just over 1% annually. Under those rules, why bother?'

Why bother, indeed. Nevertheless, any mention of reducing capital gains is habitually drowned out by an angry chorus of recriminations against the rich.

Meanwhile, those same industrial countries that tax capital gains at a lower rate than we do, or exempt them altogether, are beating us out of the gate in key areas of research and development, and in the awarding of all-important patients for new products, technologies and eventually, jobs for the future.

The real debate is not whether one American may actually profit more than another, but whether all Americans will have the equal, God-given opportunity to rise to their fullest potential in a country that rewards, rather than punishes, success, because we are a nation that is wide open to talent, and committed as we can be to winning in the world and prospering in our future.

As the prophet said in the Old Testament, Where there is no vision, the people perish. Proverbs xxix, 18

The time has come for business leaders of vision and experience who grasp the realities of meeting a payroll, creating jobs and competing in world markets, to step forward and become more active in the political process.

For, if we ever hope to make any real and permanent headway against high taxation, spending, regulation and protectionism, the battles must be fought and won in Washington, DC.

And, I am convinced Americans will rally behind men and women of principle who are willing to fight those battles — leaders who do not insult our intelligence, by pandering to us with election-year gimmicks that will never solve this Nation's problems.

The American people understand the only, true prescription for lasting prosperity is hard work, savings and investment, encouraged by policies that create opportunity and that reward initiative and success, by keeping tax and spending rates low and promoting free and unfettered trade.

And, if challenged by a clear vision and sound plan, people will come forth and deliver the long-term commitment this country must make — not for next week or even next year, but for five, ten and twenty years down the road.

We must make a long-term commitment to improving the education and skills of our children. And, that commitment should begin with greater freedom for parents to choose how and where their children are educated.

If American education is to produce more people who can compete in the economic marketplace, our schools must foster more competition in the educational market-place.

And, the principle of competition should be coupled with a commitment to train and reward outstanding teachers who will help us reach ever-higher standards of performance, backed up by rigorous testing and clear, agreed-upon guidelines with parents to enforce homework hours, and if necessary, longer school years.

As our children mature, they should be systematically exposed to the world of work and markets, and to the ways of business in other cultures, all with the aim of preparing themselves to work, compete and succeed in the global economy.

And, when these young men and women leave school, they should do so with confidence they'll not only find a challenging job, but work in the most dynamic, competitive and exciting arenas of free enterprise in the world — from our high-tech corridors to the industrial mid-west and the heartland of America, to our coastal ports, as well as our inner cities, where a drive to liberate the poor from what can accurately be called their Third World socialist, welfare state is long overdue.

And, creating that environment will require leaders in Washington who are determined to move, unswervingly, to set tax rates on labour and capital that are success and incentive-driven, to remove regulations that discourage risk and impede growth, and to use any and all means — a budget freeze, the line-item veto, the return to Gramm-Rudman, and enhanced rescission authority — to force government to live within its revenues and not permit spending to exceed the rate of growth in the economy.

Change of this dimension will require enormous, political courage. It will require the courage of men and women who, like John Templeton, understand that there is a moral foundation of freedom which rests not just upon rights, but upon responsibilities — and that our first and overriding responsibility is our duty to serve and strengthen America for the future by reigning in a government careening wildly out of control.

Thomas Jefferson warned us long ago that America must choose between economy and liberty, and profusion and servitude.

For, we ignore at our peril the age-old truth that our personal, political and economic freedoms are inextricably linked, and that when nations permit their economic freedoms to disappear, their personal and political freedoms do not long survive.

Our basic challenge, then, is to determine how much personal freedom, if any, we are willing to continue giving up in seeking collectivist security. Certainly, it is not easy to live with the uncertainties that exist in a free society, but the real personal benefits created are far superior to any other system.

It is this heritage of personal freedom that has made America a land blessed above all others. And, preserving our heritage, as men like John Templeton have laboured so long and so hard to do, is the key to an America that confidently leads the family of free nations into the 21st Century.

And I remain confident that we will.

Alistair Cooke once said that there is a great race going on in this country between vitality and decadence. I still believe in the incredible vitality of America. Decadence is not our future. I still believe that vitality will win.

This country, for all of our problems, is still the magnet for millions who risk their lives to come streaming to our shores, because we have the greatest propriety, the highest standard of living, and most important, the greatest individual freedom known to man.

And, if we embrace these responsibilities incumbent upon each of us, then we can look forward to handing over to our children, and to our children's children, an America that is more productive, more prosperous, and stronger and better — economically, financially, morally and spiritually than the one we inherited.

This is freedom's agenda, and freedom's agenda is our future agenda.

# 10

## WORLD POVERTY, TRADE AND TRICKLE DOWN

### CHARLES ELLIOTT

That this is a suitable topic for a volume of essays in honour of Sir John Templeton can hardly be in doubt. His innovative approach to portfolio investment in emerging markets has been widely hailed as one of the key breakthroughs in making new capital available to many industrialising countries, not least because his innovations have been followed by other investment houses and fund managers: there is no greater compliment than emulation.

The introduction of new capital to some of the emerging markets has come at an opportune time; at a time moreover when the argument for more market oriented macro and micro economic policies has effectively been won, and shown to have been won by the collapse of centralised planning and totalitarian dictatorship in Eastern Europe. The post debt-crisis structural adjustments which have often been the vehicle of the new economic policies in the developing world have freed up prices, privatised swathes of industry and improved the allocation of resources into the exportable sectors. The prospect of more rapid growth in such countries as Mexico, Chile, Argentina, Philippines and even Colombia has been attended both by inflows of private capital and dramatic reassessments of equity values.

In some senses, those are the success stories, or at least the on-the-way-to-success-with-a-bit-of-luck stories. There are two other stories, however, that have to be held in the right kind of creative tension with them. Both relate to the theme of the compatibility of international capital and poverty alleviation. Traditionally these have been seen as at daggers-drawn, each the antithesis of the other. It is not politically correct for the advocates of poverty alleviation to have a good word to say about the operations of international capital in whatever guise it may present itself. And, in general and apart from some rather sad window dressing, the reverse has often been the case; international capital owners have too easily dismissed the cause of poverty alleviation as soft, Leftist or best left to the voluntary sector. I shall argue in this essay that this over-polarised animosity is ill informed and overdue for reassessment. I shall do so by appealing to two areas of current interest to academic observers of international development. The first is the international setting within which would-be industrialising countries have to operate; and the second is the internal distribution of income and assets to the less than wealthy majority in all third world countries.

Most industrialising or would-be industrialising third world countries are dependent upon the export of raw materials or primary commodities in the early stages of development. Agricultural products from Argentina, coffee and beef from Brazil and Columbia, fruit and cotton from Guatemala, coffee and bauxite from Jamaica are all obvious examples from one continent: the degree of dependence on such commodities increases by an order of magnitude when the focus is shifted from the New World to Africa. It is therefore worth asking whether the international environment in which this export of commodities takes place is conducive to the growth promoting efforts of capital lenders, especially those involved in private port-folio investment — and whether it has implications for those interested in the alleviation of mass poverty.

It is now well understood that the rich countries have been paying less and less in real terms for the exports of most non-oil producing poor countries for a long time — essentially since the end of the Korean war. Long ago Hans Singer[1] and Roul Prebisch[2] gave a theoretical explanation

[1]Hans Singer: The Distribution of gains between investing and borrowing countries. *American Economic Review. Proceedings & Papers* 11.2.1950.

[2]Raul Prebisch: *Towards a Dynamic Policy for Latin America.* ON.ECLA. New York 1963.

of this process and although there have been modifications and different emphases, their main arguments have stood the test of time remarkably well. I think few people would now deny that the international commodity price system has been a powerful process whereby wealth and income have been transferred from commodity producers (not all of which are of course poor countries) to commodity importers/manufacturing exporters. This process has been reducing the import-purchasing-power of the developing countries at roughly 2% per year compounded over nearly 40 years.

The issue is so important it needs careful handling. It might be said that while prices have indeed been falling, the importing capacity of developing countries might have been increased if they had increased output. That is they could have offset lower prices by producing more. That is what European commodity producers — i.e. farmers — sometimes do, much to the chagrin of the Agriculture Commissioner in Brussels! Why should not developing countries commodity-exporties behave in the same way? And have they in fact done so?

That raises three separate questions. First can they do so? Is it the case that supply is elastic; and that marginal production will always be profitable? One cannot give one unique answer to that. Some developing countries at some periods have indeed been able to go on earning foreign exchange by expanding commodity exports despite slowly, secularly real declining prices. One thinks of Cote d'Ivoire in the 1960s and 1970s and of Malaysia on the back — the sinking back as it sadly turns out — of the palm oil boom. But equally there are plenty of countries that have not been able — or willing — to try to compensate for falling prices in this way. Sometimes this has been because of administrative hold-ups and incompetence; sometimes it has been a more rational fear that prices will in fact continue to fall and make marginal production unprofitable; and sometimes it has been difficulty in attracting capital — domestic or foreign — into sectors of production marked by a declining real international price.

The second question this argument — that countries should protect their income by increasing production to offset declining prices — raises is this; in many cases, new production comes only after substantial investment and, especially, the expenditure of desperately scarce foreign exchange. New mines need new equipment; about 60% of the cost of a new mine development in Africa will be in the form of foreign exchange. Even new plantations — of cocoa, coffee, tea, rubber — require extra fertiliser; extra transport and handling equipment; extra processing machinery. Is a country sensible to commit its scarcest single resource to the development of a crop or commodity which will possibly require repeated devaluations to keep profitable? It is, of course, a Catch 22 situation. If it expands production, it makes foreign exchange even more scarce immediately. If it does not expand production (and cannot find any other suitable export to promote), it will be even more short of foreign exchange in the future. Rock and hard place.

The third question that this raises is this: under what circumstances is it proper or appropriate or moral to expect people to run harder and harder to stay where they are? I have mentioned already farmers in this country over the last three years. It is of course a much older question than that. Kautsky called it self exploitation and he remarked how common it is among any producing group at the bottom of the power distribution — handcraft producers; small farmers; shopkeepers and market traders; all those we have come to call the informal sector. But that is the point. They are the sort of people who resort to self exploitation because they have no alternative. They are caught. It is arguably less than wise or just to recommend that to a developing country — a point to which I shall have to return.

There is a further riposte that is made by the critics of the economic performance of the Less Developed Countries.

They say that developing countries could afford to accept lower prices for their primary products if they raised labour productivity in those industries. For example, if a producer can greatly increase the productivity of labour — by shifting let us say from deep mining to open cast mining where he can use 100 ton trucks instead of labourers and their wheel barrows — is it not proper, the critics say, that some of the productivity gains (i.e. cost savings) should be shared with the consumer? This is what has happened to the prices of calculators and computers or even air fares. If, then, commodity producers have been able to offset falling prices by increasing productivity — as to a degree manufacturers have — then they have not in fact been made worse off just because prices have been falling in real terms.

This appeal to the double factorial terms of trade is theoretically unimpeachable. In fact, it is largely irrelevant. Rather few developing countries have been able to increase productivity significantly since they tend to produce tree crops — rubber, palm oil, cocoa, tea, coffee — which have proved highly resistant to technologies that would raise labour productivity. Rubber trees are still tapped now in the way Raffles would have known, except that the tapper now has a bicycle — which he wheels! But technology apart, there would be something odd about a country in which rural (albeit often disguised) unemployment was running at 20% or more spending scarce foreign exchange on machinery to make yet more people unemployed. So by all means let us look at the double factorial terms of trade — but not in the expectation that they will show a more cheerful picture than any other measure of the terms of trade.

The terms of trade remain at the root of many of the problems of the developing countries and I have tried to show that the theoretical devices by which any trading nation can deliver itself from the worst effects of a decline in the net barter terms of trade simply are not feasible in the case of the vast majority of developing commodity exporters. That makes the more sad the process by which such countries have been drawn into the trap that the declining terms of trade have come to represent. In country after country, donors, consultants, banks, investors, even Non Govermental Organisations have persuaded decision makers that the only way out of their perpetual and dire shortage of foreign exchange is to develop a thriving exporting sector — by growing bananas or palm oil or beef or flowers or oranges. . . . And as that same advice has been given to each country, the result has been yet more supply chasing very sluggish and over-supplied markets. What may have been right for one has proved disastrously wrong for many.

The World Bank and the International Monetary Fund tend to reiterate what has been Bank orthodoxy for nearly 20 years and which has been raised to a higher power in the wake of so-called structural adjustment — namely that the way developing countries spring the terms of trade trap is to add value to their commodities and sell manufactures rather than raw materials. Again, nearly unimpeachable in theory. They can point to isolated examples where it has worked — Ghanaian plywood and furniture; Indian textiles; even, for a really exotic example, fishing flies from Kenya, perhaps the greatest value ever added to a chicken feather. But this takes us into deeply debated territory. Developing countries tend to argue that they are inhibited from doing so by tariffs and non-tariff barriers, either actual or threatened. The most notorious of these is the MultiFibre Arrangement which regulates international trade in textiles and essentially shares out the world market among competing suppliers in a way that protects the interests of (inefficient) rich country producers. There are many other restrictive devices especially in the fields of agriculture and horticulture.

That general argument is then finessed in two directions. First, it is a matter of complaint among developing countries, that partially to take account of these difficulties, rich countries have set up special deals with groups of favoured developing countries which have the effect of putting at even greater disadvantage those that are excluded from the favoured circle. Thus the EEC has specially favourable arrangements for the import into the EEC of manufactured goods from the African, Caribbean and Pacific countries in association with the EEC under the terms of the various Lomé conventions. The United States has similar arrangements with countries of the Caribbean Basin — and more notoriously and in the longer term potentially hugely important is seeking to have a Free Trade Arrangement with Mexico. What does that do to, say, Ecuador or Colombia, excluded for no obvious economic reason from such arrangements, both European and American alike?

Secondly, even under such arrangements as have been made to take account of the complaints of developing countries about access to the markets of the rich countries, the benefits are fragile, unpredictable and often illusory. The Generalized System of Preferences is a case in point. As has often been said it is neither generalised, systematic or particularly preferential, increasing the value of all LDC exports by around 5%.[3] But leaving that aside, the real objection to it and to the equivalent arrangements under Lome, is that they can be set aside at very short notice (sometimes when a ship has actually left the port of loading) with no consultation and no compensation. That means that as soon as a developing country begins to use the access arrangements effectively, almost by definition they will be curtailed or withdrawn. So why take the risk; and spend the investment capital and foreign exchange in setting up an export industry which you know will soon be discriminated against?

And if the answer is that the level of tariffs is actually quite low — typically less than 12% and more usually around 6%

---

[3]Tracy Murray: How helpful is the Generalised System of Peferences to developing countries? *Economic Journal* 1973.

— we need to remember that the tariff falls on the value added alone, since the raw material is imported duty free. And as the value added is often fairly modest, the effective rate of protection is high. A third world producer has to be significantly more efficient than a first world producer if he is to compete in first world markets without tariff free access.

These justified complaints have to be balanced by the recognition that it may be inappropriate to complain about market access when the evidence is that many — indeed most — third world producers are not using the special opportunities that are extended to them under the Multifibre Arrangement or the GSP or Lomé. The problem lies on the supply side rather than on the demand side. For example one estimate of the increase in LDC exports, excluding textiles and oil, as a result of the tariff cuts in the Tokyo round, found that a zero increase was probable from five biggish LDCs and more than 5% from only two — of which one was Hong Kong. If you include textiles, the picture is very different; indeed, the trade creation effect of liberalisating the trade in textiles is greater than the effect of a 60% tariff cut on all other exports. But even in the case of textiles, the bulk of the benefit is corralled by eight countries — and over 60% of it by five.

Thus, it is a matter of some offence to the European textile industry that some developing countries sell their MFA allocations to other much more efficient producers, thus vitiating the whole *raison d'etre* of market management in favour of late starters or the economically vulnerable. To reduce domestic production to give Sri Lanka a chance to enter the international industry is one thing, so it is said; to present Sri Lanka with a windfall profit and have to compete with ultra-cheap Bangaldeshi textiles is quite another.

So we clearly need to distinguish between LDCs which are characterised by high export elasticities and those which, for whatever reason, respond only very sluggishly to export opportunities. There is of course a long and lively debate about what determines which country is which; why should Mauritius and Pakistan have been relatively success- ful exporters at least in the 1960s and 1970s while Tanzania, Ghana and Madagascar were markedly less so? I want to touch on one factor which clearly plays a pivotal role. A country that can ensure that its currency accurately reflects its production costs internationally — that is that can devalue as soon as it becomes necessary and can then forestall inflation undoing the devaluation — is in a far stronger position to develop manufactured exports than one that cannot bring off that difficult trick. And what conduces to success in that trick is a readiness to cut real incomes quite savagely and to hold them down. Now that implies one of three things — either a military dictatorship or something approximating to it; or a social system that allows one group to impose cuts on another group without the latter rioting; or a social consensus that freely accepts periodic cuts in real income as a price worth paying for industrial development in the medium term.

Seen from this perspective it is no surprise that most of the developing countries that have had elastic supply of manufactured exports fall into the first or second categor- ies — Singapore, Chile and Brazil during their military dictatorships belong to the first and South Korea, South Africa, Taiwan and Malaya (a country with one of the highest manufactured export supply elasticities in the world),[4] to the second. I can think of no developing country that exemplifies the third.

If the rationale for trying to develop manufactured ex- ports is that the terms of trade have proved unfavourable in commodities, one might then expect it to be the case — as the Bank and the Fund have always implicitly and some- times explicitly claimed — that this would not be a problem in the case of manufacturers. Since 1965, the net barter

[4]M. Davenport: *Trade Policy, Protectionism and the Third World.* London 1986.

terms of trade of developing country manufactured exports have declined by about 1% p.a. — half the rate of commodities, but, again compounded over 26 years, a serious fall.[5] LDCs have however, been able to offset that by increses in volumes; though again one has to differentiate between the strong export growers — the Tigers — and the more general case of countries in which growth has been very modest. What is also clear is that productivity in export industries has slowed markedly in the LDCs in the 1970s (as, to a lesser extent, it has in the rich countries). This implies that the factor income terms of trade in exports have declined — again not as much in commodities, but with the effect of meaning that people have to work harder and harder to be able to earn the foreign exchange to import the same volume of goods and services from overseas.

So far I have concentrated on the macro-effects; for that has been the tenor of the professional literature. Much less clearly enunciated has been the effect of declining terms of trade on real wages — and therefore on income distribution to which I shall return later. To simplify and sharpen the argument, I ignore devaluation. Consider the basic case when a developing country exporting say cocoa or shoes finds the import purchasing power of those exports falling. A smaller volume of imports can be bought. A smaller volume of exports means that in one way or another they will be rationed. Two things then happen. The domestic prices of pure imports rise; so too do prices of import intensive domestic production; and some industries using imports as inputs simply cannot get them and cease production. There is then a fall in the volume of such goods — and prices rise again. The shortage of imports has, even in the absence of devaluation, forced up the price level — and therefore cut real wages.

[5]P. Sarkar & Hans Singer: Manufactured exports of developing countries and the terms of trade since 1965. *World Development.* 19.4.1991.

The poverty effect of that is that it is people on the margins of employment who get squeezed out of jobs. Lower real wages lead to lower employment. The people at the bottom suffer both ways. In some countries that process reaches the rural areas. The cost of agricultural inputs — especially fuel and fertilisers — may rise and so food prices rise. Falling urban employment may well lead to urban-rural migration, with the result that money wages of rural workers fall. As food prices are rising and money wages falling, the real wages of one of the poorest groups in the country — unskilled rural employees — fall fast.

If, to take one empirical example of this process at work, we compare the net barter terms of trade of the Philippines (all exports; commodities and manufacturers both) with real wages, we find that real wages follow the terms of trade almost perfectly. Both fell, with some irregularity, by just over 50% between 1955 and 1980 — and then went on falling.[6]

I labour this point because while it has been well known since Singer/Prebisch that the terms of trade shifted income from rich to poor countries, it has not been adequately understood that the people on whom that process tends to fall most sharply is wage earners and farmers — in general, some of the poorer, and sometimes amongst the poorest, people of all — and that without even taking into account the effects of repetitive devaluations which constantly declining terms of trade tend to bring in their wake.

We have there, then, a strange combination of effects. On the one hand, the international setting of the economies of poor countries makes them poorer and makes the poorest people within them still more poor. At the same time, the international setting also makes growth impossible or nearly impossible, partly by reducing the domestic capital available and partly by reducing the capacity of the government

[6]P. W. Mathur: *Why developing countries fail to develop. Economic Framework and Economic Subordination.* London 1991.

to provide the basic infra-structural services to which international capital tends now to give more significance than low wages alone. This suggests that whereas those of us who are concerned about poverty in the Third World are often invited to regard international capital owners/managers as opposed to our concerns, there is, in the drastic reform of the international trading system, a surprising degree of common ground. For all the present emphasis among donors, from the World Bank to bilateral donors like the British Overseas Development Administration, on the role that aid can and should play in poverty alleviation, the larger fact is that as long as poverty alleviating projects are set in the context of the present international trading system, they will be unsuccessful in attaining their goals to any significant degree. In an exactly analogous way, injections of private capital into those third world countries that are rapped in the present trading system will not be as growth-promoting as they could and should be. Poverty alleviation and capital accumulation are twin victims of the same structural fault.

Can the same be true when we switch attention from the international arena to domestic issues of internal income distribution? Again it is often alleged that there is a polarity between those who are concerned with poverty and who therefore wish to see income re-distributed to the poor on the one hand; and on the other those who, in the interests of the profitability of capital, wish to see income accrue to the providers of productive resources. Let us approach this question by reviewing some of the effects of the liberalisation policies I mentioned at the beginning of this essay.

My reading of the data is that in most countries there has been a remarkable collapse in the ability of particular groups — what in an earlier literature was called the aristocracy of labour — to protect their real incomes. Civil servants, skilled manual workers, professionals; these were the people who did rather well in the 1960s and much of the 1970s. The debt crisis; the terms of trade; and latterly the economic reforms initiated by the IMF and the World Bank have effectively smashed their protected status in the labour market.

But that has happened in the context of economic collapse — or something very close to that — usually associated with high levels of inflation. In that process and the reforms that follow it, there has tended to be a shift in the factor distribution of income from labour to capital; and in the sector distribution from domestic good and service producers towards the producers of tradeables and food. Leaving aside the successful Newly Industralised Countries, then, it is hard to see trickle down operating in the way the glib have traditionally assumed. There has been redistribution — and some of that redistribution has been 'down' the income range; towards farmers, including, in some countries, quite small farmers. But some has not. It has been to capital employed in the export sector and to a much lesser degree to labour (usually fairly skilled labour) in that sector. Richer farmers, richer exporters — and often significantly poorer artisans and petit bourgeoisie; and very, very poor urban unemployed.

The orthodox response to that analysis would be to say that the success of the presently successful is the way to expand the economy and thus improve the poverty of the rest. Another run for trickle down. It may happen; there are some cases where it seems to be doing so on a very limited scale already, in some of the Latin American relative success stories — Chile, Argentina — perhaps on quite a significant scale. But it will only happen on two conditions that have emerged from our earlier analysis; that it happens very slowly (so that real wages do not force costs up too fast) and that the markets for exports turn out to be enduring. On neither side does there seem room for excessive optimism.

To raise another issue, it used to be said that developing countries manifested urban bias. One sense of that was that urban dwellers did not pay enough for their food. Richer townies meant poorer farmers. Many countries addressed that issue in the 1980s, again prodded by the IMF. The evidence tends to suggest, however, that a decisive shift in the farmers' terms of trade have proved difficult to make stick. Familiar reportage of food riots illustrates one result of trying to raise food prices. That is the tip of an iceberg — or rather of a volcano. You can do it once — and survive. You may be able to do it twice and get away with it. But in anything that has any pretence of a democracy, it is hard to go on doing it month after month, inflationary year after inflationary year — especially when you can keep the lid on food prices by the back door, by accepting food aid from the surpluses of the West. Urban bias is dead; long live urban bias.

Since the redistribution with growth debates of the 1970s — that now look so dusty and jejune — one aspect of income distribution has been given proper prominence; access by poor or relatively poor people to productive assets. The most obviously appropriate productive asset is land. Is it the case that access to productive assets by poor people has become easier; or have the rich squeezed out the poor? In the post debt crisis/structural adjustment period, it is hard to be optimistic. Indeed two ways in which the debt crisis has been handled — through debt for equity swaps and through privatisation — have had exactly the reverse effect; they have transferred assets not just to the domestic elite (the shareholders of large conglomerates in some Latin American countries) but, for the most part, to foreigners.

At the more modest level at which poor people tend to operate, two almost universal features have made it very hard for them to acquire and keep productive assets. The first is inflation, which as always has tended to favour borrowers — not usually poor people — and the second is the critical shortage of foreign exchange. In so far as even poor people are dependent upon imported intermediate goods to make their assets productive — oil, fertiliser, machinery — they have been caught in this bind. I do not deny occasional successes — the Bramiputra programme in Malaysia may be one; just possibly Zimbabwean land reform will prove, against the flow of history, to be another — but I think optimism in this area is misplaced. Richer asset owners may have had a torrid time; some may have lost their assets to foreigners; but they have had a better time than most poor non-asset owners.

In this case, then, it seems reasonable to conclude that the interests of international capital owners are not identical with those of the poor; indeed over a large spectrum of experience and policy, they conflict. But need it be so?

Perhaps a fundamental distinction will help clarify the issues before us. If the international capital owner sees it as in his or her interest to keep wages low; to keep food prices down (and thus reinforce urban bias); to concentrate income flows in the upper deciles of the income distribution, then clearly there is an inevitable conflict between those interests and poverty alleviation. But the international capital owner need not necessarily take such a view. She may decide that her interests demand a widening of the domestic market, which implies raising disposable incomes much further down the income scale. She may also decide that in the long run the best way to maintain high productivity is not through the short run pursuit of low wages, but through the release onto the labour market of increasingly highly skilled workers in such numbers as to prevent the emergence of labour bottle necks. And if she takes the quality of labour seriously, this will commit her to a wide range of social expenditure in the health, education, womens' rights and housing fields.

In general it is surely the case that the narrow, short-run opportunism of the mobile screw driver plant, highly dependent as it was on cheap labour; and largely uncommitted as it was to the domestic market for goods or labour-inputs, has passed its peak. That such plants still exist and that they will continue to be a feature of the operations of international capital in some countries — Mexico under a free trade pact with the US is an obvious example — cannot be denied. But the recent trends have been away from these operations, and if the current self-questioning in Japan about the absorptive capacity of the consumer markets of Europe and the US for electronic consumer goods may be taken as a straw in the wind, the tendency to see the domestic market and its expansion as key to the survival of international capital in the Third World is likely to be reinforced. To that extent the interests of international capital are likely to become more aligned with poverty alleviation; more aligned but never, or at least not in the foreseeable future, identical. For the point of poverty alleviation is to put income streams and/or assets in the hands of the very poorest on the ground that theirs is the most pressing need. The market widening interests of international capital will favour increasing productive resources and skills in the second or third quartiles of the income distribution. For the rest, reliance will have to be placed on the trickle down or charity.

In conclusion, one of John Templeton's great assets has been his ability over the years to challenge received wisdoms in a wide range of fields. One received wisdom that needs challenge is the convention that international capital, including private portfolio investment, is hostile to the interests of the poor of the world. I have tried to show that those who are concerned about the plight of the poorest need to be more concerned about the terms of trade and all that follows from their tendency to turn against the developing world — and in that concern to make common cause with owners of international capital who seek a decent return in the third world in compensation for the enhanced risks they accept. On the more delicate subject of domestic income distribution, I have acknowledged that there are direct conflicts and that the processes of structural adjustment have exacerbated some of these. But I concluded the argument by suggesting that we may well be entering a new phase, especially in Latin America and Asia, where the concurrence of interest may be not perfect, but at least approximate. I wish I could believe that to be likely to be true of Africa too. That may have to wait until not the next generation, but the one after that.

[Some of this material was included in a lecture given to the Royal Society of Arts to mark the 50th anniversary of Oxfam. That lecture was subsequently published in the Journal of the RSA and, independently, by Oxfam. The author and editor acknowledge the kindness of the RSA and Oxfam in permitting the inclusion in this article of that material.]

## POSTSCRIPT

The following chapter was published 20 years ago in a book called *The money Managers,* and is republished here by kind permission of the author, John Train.

It is interesting to note what Sir John was thinking then.

# TO EVERYTHING THERE IS A SEASON

## JOHN TRAIN

One day in 1939, just after war had broken out in Europe, a young man named John Templeton called his broker at Fenner & Beane and gave one of the oddest and most annoying orders a broker could ever hope to receive.

'I want you to buy me a hundred dollars' worth of every single stock on both major exchanges that is selling for no more than one dollar a share.'

The broker might have refused the order, which was a nightmare to execute and a most unsatisfactory way to earn a negligible commission, except that Templeton had worked for him as a trainee two years earlier.

After a while he reported that he had bought Templeton a hundred dollars' worth of every stock on either exchange that was not entirely bankrupt.

'No, no,' said Templeton, 'I want them *all*. Every last one, bankrupt or not.' Grudgingly the broker went back to work and finally completed the order. When it was all over, Templeton had bought a junkpile of 104 companies in roughly $100 lots, of which 34 were bankrupt. He held each stock for an average of four years before selling. The result was no joke at all: he got over $40,000 for the kit — four times his cost.

Some of the transactions were startling. He bought Standard Gas $7 Preferred at $1 and sold it at $40. He bought 800 shares of Missouri Pacific Preferred - in bankruptcy — at 12 cents and eventually sold out at $5. (It eventually went over $100: had he sold at the top, that particular $100 would have turned not into $4,000 but $80,000!)

A singular aspect of this transaction was that Templeton didn't have $10,000 in cash. He was convinced that stocks were dirt cheap, and that of them all the neglected cats and dogs selling for less than $1 were the best values. When the war started in Europe he reasoned that, if anything, was going to pull America out of its economic slump, and virtually all stocks would rise. So he had gone to his boss and borrowed the entire amount.

John Templeton was poor. He came from Winchester, Tennessee. During the Depression, while he was in his second year at Yale, his father told him that he couldn't give him any more money for his education. So Templeton worked his way through college, with the aid of scholarships. After that he won a Rhodes scholarship and went to Oxford for two years, seeing Europe during his vacations. Then he came back to Tennesee and eventually went to New York, first as a trainee at Fenner & Beane, one of the predecessors of Merril Lynch, and after that in a seismic exploration company.

There he was then World War II began and he became convinced that the ten-year slump in stock prices was over and everything would boom — especially the Cinderellas that nobody considered as suitable investment.

That one extraordinary transaction set the pattern for Templeton's later ones.

First, *he insisted on buying only what was being thrown away.*

Second, *he held the stocks he had bought for an average of four years.*

That usually gives a bargain enough time to be recognised, so you can make the big revaluation when a stock moves to a higher multiple of higher earnings, the 'double-play' profit. (Of course, you completely miss the 21 year run of the great growth stock in its prime, which for most investors is their best hope of stock market profits. There are very few Templetons who succeed in buying undiscovered values and selling them again in a four-year cycle.)

After his coup Templeton had some money, so two years later, when he learned that an elderly investment counsellor wanted to retire and sell his business, which had only eight clients, he wrote him a cheque for $5,000 and took over the firm. The clients stayed, but eight isn't many, so Templeton had a bad time of it at first, and had to live off his savings. Then, however, word of his abilities began to spread, and he has never lacked for clients — or income — since.

His firm — Templeton, Dobbrow & Vance — eventually grew to manage $300 million, including eight mutual funds. The trouble was that having so many different clients, left Templeton working so hard that he didn't have time enough to think. Finally he and his associates sold their firm to Piedmont Management, keeping only Templeton Growth Fund, which Piedmont didn't want because it was based in Canada and couldn't be distributed in the United States.

At fifty-six, John Templeton started all over again. He resolved first that he would never let himself get so busy that he ran out of time. Not only time to think about investments but also to reflect on the larger world, particularly the various approaches to religion. So he moved to Nassau, and on the grounds of the Lyford Cay Club built a white house in the southern style, with columns on all four sides. There he assembled his securities files and started giving his attention to managing his one tiny remaining fund, of which he and some of his old clients owned most of the shares. The record of this fund in the next years proved that John Templeton is one of the great investors.

Over the 20 years ending 31 December 1978, a $1,000 investment in his fund became worth about $20,000, if all distributions had been reinvested in more shares — which made it the top performer of all funds.

Even more impressive, in each of the preceding seven years his has been the top quarter of all funds, and some computations by *Fundscope* have put Templeton both among the top 20 funds (out of more than 400) in making money in rising markets and the top five in not losing it in down markets. I am particularly impressed by the latter achievement, since the most decline-resistant funds include some that are permanently in bonds. To give an idea of the singularity of this record, the much larger T. Rowe Price New Horizons Fund, which also buys secondary companies and does spectacularly in rising markets, ranks more than 200 places behind Templeton in down markets. In a word, Templeton's consistency can only be described as phenomenal.

To be fair, one should compare his result only with other small, international portfolios that are not concerned with owning 'big names'. The manager of a $1 billion domestic pension fund has a far tougher job than the manager of a small, uninhibited account. It is the *QE II* compared to an ocean racer.

In the first place, the small size of Templeton Growth Fund obviously gave him a flexibility not enjoyed by the managers of 50 to 100 times as much money. A $100,000 commitment in the stock of a small company can substantially affect his fund's performance if it doubles. Also, he can and does sell stocks and raise cash when he gets edgy, which the largest funds almost never do. He sometimes moves 50 per cent into reserves, although he says he has little ability to recognise tops and bottoms in the market — a trait he shares with most of the top stock-pickers.

Then, his investment selections range over many markets. He is quite as much at home in the Japanese and Canadian exchanges as in American exchanges, and knows those of Switzerland, Germany, Holland, Belgium, Australia and South Africa.

Finally, and perhaps most important of all, he does not need to stick to large, familiar names: what trust companies wrongly call 'quality'. An established small specialty company with fat profit margins selling for a low price-earnings ratio is often a safer investment — if you are sure you have the facts right — than a huge, mediocre, heavily unionised and regulated standard industrial that sells at a high price because everybody knows about it. Templeton will go into dozens of little companies his clients have never heard of, and is prepared to buy almost all the stock available. Managers of large portfolios avoid smaller companies. They fear, rightly, on the whole, that they don't know enough about them. If they are dealing in big numbers, taking the time to master small situations won't pay.

Incidentally, the willingness to invest in many countries ties in with a willingness to buy 'junior' stocks. Quite often the smaller, cheaper, faster-growing company is outside the US. For instance, Safeway sells at about eight times earnings, and will do well to maintain a 15% growth rate in the future. Within the food-chain sector, Templeton, instead, bought Ito Yokado, the best-managed and second largest supermarket chain in Japan, at ten times earnings, growing more than 30% a year. He points out that in Japan supermarkets, which are a direct bridge between the producer and the consumer, are still in their infancy, and have decades to grow before they are as common as they are here.

Real estate provides another example. Templeton considers it a field of perennial interest in an inflationary era. Having looked at real estate companies in Japan and England — where property companies enjoy great favour with investors — he discovered that the Canadian market offers better bargains than either. Once he had decided to invest in Canadian real estate, he chose a package of companies that almost no American investor — even a professional — would have heard of: Abbey Glen Property, Daon Development, S. B. McLaughlin Associates, and Nu-West Development, all bought at between two and four times cash flow per share; also Allarco, at five times earnings (which, however, he thinks will triple). A willingness to invest in smaller companies further implies great diversification among stocks. The fund's portfolio not long ago contained 220 different names.

Still, the advantages of internationalism, small size, and diversification into secondary names only set the stage for superior performance. They don't bring it about.

What is Templeton's technique? How does he do it?

His basic philosophy can be stated in one sentence:

*Search among many markets for the companies selling for the smallest fraction of their true worth.*

He is not content to buy a bargain. It must be the *best* bargain. Of course, many seeming bargains are nothing of the sort. So when he finds one, he studies it, restudies it, and only buys the stock when he is convinced the values are authentic. Even then, he ruefully admits, he makes constant mistakes. They are inevitable. But because he is heavily diversified, the damage is limited.

*The best bargains will be in stocks that are completely neglected, that other investors are not even studying.* That, of course, explains the proliferation of unfamiliar names in his portfolio.

'Look it over,' he said to me, with his usual bland smile. 'I'll bet you don't know more than a third of them.' I did a bit better, but not much. And a number of the companies I was familiar with were on his list for reasons I didn't immediately think of.

For instance, Wells, Rich, Greene. Most people in the business world know about Mary Wells and her success in building up one of the 'hot' advertising agencies of the 1960s. But to *invest* in an ad agency — a collection of prima donnas in one of the most volatile and personal of all businesses? Unthinkable! When the agencies went public in the late 1960s I wrote of it as a typical bull-market blowoff phenomenon: outsiders willing, in essence, to pay the insiders their peak salaries in advance for the next ten or 15 years and still hoping to make something for themselves out of the investment. Basically, it's impossible — you can't invest in a profession. If things go well, the insiders will want to increase their take.

That's how it worked out with Wells, Rich, Greene. The insiders sold $14 million — 690,000 shares out of 1.6 million outstanding — in two public issues at about 20 when things were booming. The stock eventually got up to 28. Then times got rough and the stock drifted down to $5. I observed all this with gloomy satisfaction. What you'd expect, I said to myself: never invest in a profession.

Then, however, came a twist. With the stock at $6, Mrs Wells and her colleagues offered to buy it all back. They offered paper with a real value of about $9 a share, as against a book value of $11 a share. They were able to buy back and retire 1,632,000 shares this way, leaving only 464,000 outstanding (plus 400,000 reserved for options). The original buyers at $20 who sold out again had parted with half their money.

About this point the Templeton Fund bought 25,000 shares — almost all the 'float' left in the market — at $8, which meant that on average it paid even less than the company itself did. Templeton feels that with the smaller number of shares and better conditions, earnings per share could well triple. If so, the fund's purchase would work out at less than twice earnings. Thanks to the reduced amount of stock, book value went back to $20 per share, which is what the fund sold it for.

At some time almost anything is likely to become a bargain, if you're in a position to evaluate the neglected factor that will change things for the better. To perceive this factor you have to wear glasses different from those worn by others who don't like what they see. Templeton thinks that the investor needs this ability to recognise unfamiliar values more than any other skills. He calls it flexibility.

*A flexible viewpoint is the professional investor's greatest need, and will be increasingly needed in the future.*

Templeton has several of the same concerns about the future of investments that I do.

He is always attentive to the tendency toward direct or disguised expropriation in a given country — what he calls socialism. Not only outright takeovers, but price controls*

* He agrees with "Train's Law" — *Price Controls Increase Prices* (by reducing production). How slow mankind has been to learn this simple truth, and how expensive it has been. Rent control has done as much as anything to wreck New York City.

and other entanglements that inhibit business and destroy the investor's incentive.

*Always ask yourself whether a company is in an industry that's a natural candidate to be socialised.* The answer should be sought on a worldwide basis. For instance, in almost all countries banks are a natural target of government intervention. So are mining companies. Otherwise, copper mines would be interesting, since the price of the metal is rising.

Templeton offered women's hats as a perfect regulation-proof industry. I replied that through the years the Romans and others tried to regulate the excesses of women's clothes through sumptuary laws — generally without success. Templeton was entertained by my observation that Tampax seemed an unlikely subject of regulation: one could scarcely conceive of Teddy Kennedy rising on the Senate floor to excoriate the profiteers behind this humble device: 'I have here in my hand . . .' (Even Tampax has in fact been the subject of an attempt at price regulation in the UK. There the government suggested that the margins were too high.)

Templeton cites Josten's Inc. as a company that should not be a natural target of regulation. It is America's leading maker of high-school class rings, and has a strong position in academic diplomas, caps and gowns, and yearbooks. It has had steadily rising earnings for 21 years; sales have quadrupled and earnings per share almost tripled over the last ten years.

He points out that hotel-room prices are less subject to control than residential rents. Templeton has owned several hotel companies; Commonwealth Holiday Inns, Four Seasons Hotels and Skyline Hotels — all Canadian — and United inns of Atlanta. In all real estate transactions the buyer looks at cash flow — earnings plus depreciation — rather than at plain earnings. United Inns is still only 3.5 times cash flow.

Newspaper chains, I observed, some of which are money machines and ideal monopolies, are regulation-resistant. Freedom of the press!

*The other great problem is inflation,* which Templeton expects to accelerate in the future. A company must be able to cope with inflation to be a sound investment. Advertising agencies have this ability, he observes: their income is a percentage of the customer's gross advertising outlay, so as prices go up their income rises accordingly. Eventually most countries will have to switch to inflation accounting, which shows what a company is doing in real terms, not just in nominal dollars; when that happens, the earnings of companies with high debt loads will at least double as they are seen to be repaying their bondholders with depreciating currency. Electric utility companies will be prime beneficiaries of this restatement of earnings, but are so heavily regulated as to be unattractive investments anyway.*

Debt-ridden real estate companies are, on the contrary, excellent speculations during an inflation. They are thoroughly unpopular: despised, in fact, except in England and Japan. The UK property companies, for no good reason, sell for more than twice their Canadian counterparts, and the Japanese companies for more than three times.

Another hedge against inflation that Templeton likes is shopping centres. Ordinarily the leases between the landlord and the operator are specifically drawn to offset inflation, and provide for escalation of payments according to a formula linked to turnover. If the supermarket's volume rises, so does the rent it pays to the owner of the centre. While Templeton does not hold stock in shopping centre companies at the moment, he mentioned General Growth Companies as a major owner, along with E. W. Hahn, a California-based operation.

Listening to Templeton emphasise the importance of trying to see the values that the public is overlooking I was reminded of Hemingway's advice that at the moment of climactic action a writer should take his attention from the

---

* Another possibility might be higher taxes on the restated profits, and thus even less cash for the companies.

main event — the terero going in over the horns, or the
boxer flooring his opponent — and study the crowd, lost in
its own emotion, unconscious of itself. Wilhelm Reich talks
of the importance of listening with the 'third ear': behind
the self-centred babble of the patient there often emerges
a quite different, simpler pattern — the real message, the
essential truth of the situation, of which the speaker is
unaware, and for which the therapist should always be
listening. But how does the investor escape from the unend-
ing static of 'news' and opinion, the surge and ebb of the
passions of the crowd?

One answer is experience. After 30 years of getting a
bloody nose every time he jumps on a bandwagon, even the
most enthusiastic investor attains some measure of detach-
ment from the crowd's enthusiasm and desperations.

Templeton has gone a lot further, though, to make it as
easy as possible for him to keep his perspective. The distance from his large, cool, porticoed white house on its little
hill overlooking the grounds of Lyford Cay to the roar and
shouting of the floor of the stock exchange is measured in
psychological light-years. The house itself and everything in
it are a silent reproach to excitement and hyperactivity.

Templeton himself, a spare, neat man, even in that warm
climate carefully dressed in pale lime-coloured trousers
and a striped lemon-coloured jacket with a neat striped tie,
would be, one knows at once, the last man in Christendom
to fall victim to some ephemeral enthusiasm. As he drives
slowly in his blue Rolls from his house to the club to have a
light lunch with a Canadian banker, is his soul full of
passionate yearnings to catch a one-week move in some
over-the-counter speculation — an above-ground swim-
ming pool company, perhaps, or a highly-promoted mining
venture? Scarcely.

Does he worry about the ambitions of his number four
man, or whether his staff is getting lazy or the overhead is
getting out of hand? Scarcely. He has a staff of one, plus two
secretaries.

Does he spend feverish days on the telephone, getting the latest gossip from brokers, the latest news off the broad tape, and the jokes going around the floor? Scarcely. The brokers are told to send him in writing what they think he'd like to see; not to call.

Does he worry about each week's sales of the fund, and have intense meetings with the sales manager? Scarcely. He lives in Nassau but the fund's office is in Canada and the sales organisation is in St Petersburg, Florida: one imagines that they are not encouraged to call him day and night with small problems.

The whole *mise en scene* helps Templeton to do his job.

Templeton has endowed a prize for progress in religion which is awarded annually in London. Its value, about £80,000, has enabled it to attract the interest and support of eminent people. Templeton hopes that the award will help focus attention on the life and work of the recipients, who have included Mother Theresa of Calcutta and Brother Roger of the Taize Community.

He compares spiritual growth to gardening. 'If you find a weed,' he says, 'you go out and get rid of it. The same for a bad thought or a bad emotion.'*

I asked him if good works and nonattachment to material things figured in spiritual development.

'Works *come* from spiritual development,' he said. 'If you start with the works you move to humanism, a very different thing.'

As to non-attachment, he doesn't believe in it at all. He is attached to many things, including the stock market.

The Lyford Cay Club floats in space, financially speaking. Its 950 members are drawn from more than two dozen countries, and the tone is far more English than American. One has no predisposition to think automatically in terms

---

* I tried on him the Buddhist paradox: "The mind of Buddha is steeped in corruption, sin, and death." The point is that to God no created thing is alien: our weed may be God's orchid. Templeton seemed unimpressed.

of American stocks, as a portfolio manager in Minneapolis would, or of European stocks, as would one in Hamburg. The investment scene as viewed from Nassau resembles a coral reef perceived through a glass-bottomed boat: you float by and study what seems interesting, without being anchored to one spot or another. Templeton's remoteness being anchored to one spot or another. Templeton's remoteness certainly helps him reflect judiciously on the risks and rewards in the various countries he is prepared to invest in.

Another advantage to Lyford Cay, surprisingly enough, is Templeton's access to first-hand information. A portfolio manager in New York is likely to have contacts with other portfolio managers and with stockbrokers, who themselves have limited information and are always trying to sell him things. The population of Lyford Cay, on the other hand, is made up of successful industrialists from many parts of the world — they have to be, to pay the dues — and their guests. They have come to the sum on vacation to enjoy themselves. One can exchange opinions with them easily in that attractive ambience, much more easily than would be likely in an office visit on a tight schedule.

Templeton has far broader sources of information than this, of course. Almost 30 years ago he was a founder of the Young President's Organisation, which now had thousands of members and former members around the world. He was also a president of the Chief Executives' Forum, a sort of YPO alumni association, which meets twice a year. Through his acquaintances in the YPO old-boy network he says he has access to about 500 presidents and top managers of every sort of business.

These sources, added to the knowledge and contacts built up in 40 years of investing, mean that Templeton can count on being able to develop primary sources of information on almost any company he finds interesting.

How does Templeton decide which are the countries to invest in and which are not?

Obviously, the ones to avoid are those which have conditions that make investment difficult or impossible: socialism and inflation. The two go together. Either stifles growth.

For years Templeton has favoured Japan, and historically perhaps the most striking thing about his fund, after its interest in small 'special situations', has been its concentration of investment in that country, which reached a peak of 60% in 1970, and has fallen to 10% in 1979, in response to the rise in the Tokyo stock market together with the fall in the US market.

Even now, says Templeton, over the next ten years Japan should have much less tendency toward socialism than the United States and, perhaps for that very reason, about twice the growth rate.

In 1962, when Templeton first got interested in Japan, one could buy the leading companies at two or three times real earnings, with the benefit of extensive hidden assets that didn't appear on the balance sheet. American and European investors just couldn't believe their eyes, so the bargains persisted year after year: pharamaceutical companies growing 30% per year and selling for a third of the multiples of the comparable US companies.

Today, the growth rates are slowing down in Japan, although they are still higher than in the USA, but more important for the investor, the values have been recognised, so the prices are no longer the bargains that they were. Templeton says, therefore, that he is slowly cutting down his exposure to Japan and moving back to the US, which, he finds, is the other most profitable place to put his money.

We discussed some specific Japanese companies that Templeton finds attractive. Templeton says that of all the companies he owns, Ito Yokado, the supermarket chain, is the one he has most confidence for the long term. It should maintain a 30% growth rate for a good ten years. Supermarkets are just getting started there. It now sells over 20 times earnings, but with such brilliant prospects it's well worth it.

I asked him about Toto, which dominates the bathroom fixtures market in Japan — where few houses have bathrooms. Templeton said he preferred Takara Standard, in a similar line of business. The Japanese have traditionally had wooden kitchen installations, and are just catching on to the American style of Formica and metal counters, cabinets and sinks which are easier to build and keep clean. Takara Standard has 89% of this market. Like Tot, it has depots all over the country and so can make rapid and cheap deliveries to any point. A new company entering either field has trouble delivering these heavy installations to different cities rapidly and cheaply.

Templeton points out that when he first invested in Japan 20 years ago, Japanese investors liked the big names because they had heard of them, and so would pay more for a stranded whale — the Japanese equivalent of an Allied Chemical, Chrysler, or Westinghouse — than for a specialty growth company in its dynamic phase. They also give more weight to the six-month earnings outlook than to the six-year prospects. Now, however, the smaller companies sell at a substantial premium over the giants.

The entire Japanese stock market — which is measured by an index called, in a spirit of flattering imitation, the Dow Jones Average — now stands over 27 times earnings. What bargains there are in the Japanese market are found among the growth stocks.

Thus Matsushita, says Templeton, has a 15% earnings growth prospect as far as the eye can see, and yet the Japanese will only pay nine times earnings for it because of shorter-term uncertainties. He says that Matsushita might be his second choice from his list of Japanese companies as a long-term holding.

Nissan Motors, makers of Datsun, he once found far more attractive than its American counterpart, Ford. Both companies are less vertically integrated than General Motors. Ford should continue to be highly profitable, but is unlikely to grow as fast as the average US company. Nissan, on the contrary, should be the fastest-growing car company in the world — at a rate of perhaps 15% a year, unless the yen remains overpriced. It is the principal imported car in the US. Its competitor Toyota has a larger turnover in yen, but lower unit sales, and does not enjoy Nissan's greatest strength, outstandingly able management. On the other hand, in 1979, Templeton found Ford, at three times reported 1978 earnings, a much better buy than Nissan at 15 times. Bridgestone Tire, Japanese in spite of its name, has sales of about $1 billion a year and controls most of the Japanese tire market, as though Goodyear, Firestone, and Goodrich had been able to beat down anti-trust constraints and form one huge, dominant concern.

Among the Japanese stockbrokers he finds both Yamachi Securities and Daiwa Securities most helpful: penetrating, thorough, and till improving.

Besides Japan, the US, and Canada, Templeton considers only a few areas suitable for investment: Germany, Switzerland, the northern European countries, Spain, Australia, and New Zealand (the last two of which have at least for the moment shaken off the socialist virus), Hong Kong and Singapore. South Africa's social tensions imply to Templeton that, to be attractive, a stock there should be twice as favourably price as one in, say, Germany. He finds Brazil of great potential interest, once its present restrictions on foreign investments are removed.

He has a few outstanding sources of information for non-Japanese foreign securities, but since the true facts are not publicly available he still has to depend on industry scuttle-but, insiders' tips, and bankers' indiscretions. He considers Harry G. A. Seggerman, of Fidelity Pacific Fund, to be a very skilful investor in foreign companies, apparently using methods similar to Templeton's own. I asked him if he made a practice of studying portfolios of other funds as a source of ideas. 'I do indeed,' he replied. 'I follow about 20 of them, and every time the reports come out I go over them carefully to see what they've been able to think up.'

While Templeton has tried venture capital investing, his experiences have been unsatisfactory; he was giving far more time to his stable of new ventures than their place in his portfolio justified.

Early in his career Templeton made hundreds of personal visits to companies, going through the plants and sizing everything up. In recent years, however, he has rarely found this necessary.

He has a standard list of questions he likes to ask management:

One of the first is *'Do you have a long-range plan?'*

Then, *'What will be your average annual growth rate?'*

If the target growth rate is higher than the historical one, he asks, *'Why should the future be different from the past? What are your problems?'*

And then, a key point, *'Who is your ablest competitor?'* and the essential, *'Why?'*

Finally, a question that Templeton finds particularly enlightening, *'If you couldn't own stock in your own company, which of your competitors would you want to invest in . . . and why?'*

As you find out fast enough in security analysis, contact with a single company can mislead as much as inform. Management is obviously going to blow its own trumpet. If you visit most of the companies in an industry over a period of many years, you eventually develop an informed concept of the entire group. You learn which sources are reliable, which managements achieve their objectives, which company officers tend to make exaggerated claims. Particularly, even a few minutes with a company's chief competitor or a major supplies may be vastly instructive. Your informant can tell what he knows about a competitor, while he is not permitted to divulge inside information about his own company. Even if he does, the investor can be punished for using it. Also, of course, he will probably speak more impartially about the outside company.

Templeton also makes extensive use of secondary sources, and indeed relies much more on the figures than on firsthand impressions. Perhaps his most important source is the great panorama of facts in *The Value Line Investment*

*Survey* (not the opinions, which are half-baked). By working one's way through the 15-odd-year history of such elements as sales, profit margins, depreciation, working capital, and all the rest one can grasp most of what is essential about the life of an enterprise.

Templeton also finds the *Wall Street Transcript* — which reproduces dozens of brokers' reports on companies each week — a valuable aid. To maintain his files, which he keeps in an office in a tiny shopping centre just outside the gates of the Lyford Cay Club, he used to need a librarian. Now, he says, he can find the answers to most questions by looking up the company in the index of the *Transcript.*

He makes wide use of brokers, but only for establishing facts, paying no attention to their buy and sell recommendations. Almost no brokers — less than 1%, he judges — think in his terms. (Similarly, he doubted that even one Swiss banker was considering the variations of real estate values between England and Canada that he found so interesting.) Over the years Templeton has learned what brokerage sources are likely to be useful to him for collecting facts. He instantly discards everything else.

A paradox of collecting for profit — whether stocks, works of art, real estate, or anything else — is that the best buy can never be what the dealer or gallery is pushing at the time. A notable book collector — Philip Hofer of the Houghton Library at Harvard — has told me that one of his most successful approaches in visiting a dealer is to ask: *'What do you have that you don't want?'* That volume will usually be covered with dust in the cellar, and if of real quality is likely to be a far better buy than the 'special' in the window, which will perforce be marked up to what a dealer thinks a passerby will pay for it.

Similarly, if a stock is so out of favour that there are virtually no buyers — that is, it practically can't be sold — a broker who has to pay a lot of overhead and support his salesmen can't afford to get involved with it; least of all a stock with a small float. Thus the bargain-hunting investor will always tend to be on his own, unable to rely on others for ideas, as distinct from facts.

Templeton's portfolio represents what he thinks are the best buys in marketable securities anywhere in the world — giving full consideration to the safety of the countries where they are found.

*Once a stock has moved up and no longer is a bargain, then if he finds a much better buy, out goes the first one.*

He always uses this comparison-shopping approach to investments.

I asked him if he made any effort to buy stocks just as they are emerging from the wilderness, as investment interest picks up.

He replied that he had only recently begun to give weight to that factor. Throughout his career he had always been able to be patient — perhaps too patient, he now thinks. So: *if one of two otherwise similar stocks is just starting to attract interest and the other is still in eclipse, then he gives preference to the one that is starting to move.*

In his analytical approach, Templeton starts by trying to determine the intrinsic value of a company. In the mid-1940s his investment counsel firm did as much as any to apply Graham's original, full-scale technique systematically — the analysis of companies through careful study of their significant financial ratios in the hope of establishing true values. The drudgery that this entailed has now been much alleviated by such services as *Value Line*, where for $300 a year you have easily available most of the information that an office full of analysts assembled for you in the old days less promptly and less accurately.

So now, Templeton says, he almost never has to do basic financial analysis himself. For US, Canadian, and Japanese companies it's available for a fee, and for other foreign companies it's almost impossible, because the published figures aren't real. You have to find out what you can by asking questions. There are 100 or so factors that can well be considered in making an appraisal, although not all are appropriate to any given enterprise. Thus, in studying a natural resources company you might omit perhaps a quarter of the possible factors, for a manufacturing company, a different quarter.

About six factors are crucial, and universally applicable to every situation.

1. *The price-earnings ratio.*
2. *Operating profit margins.*
3. *Liquidating value.*
4. The company's *growth* rate gets a lot of weight, and particularly the *consistency* of earnings growth. If a company's growth falters for one year, that may be all right. If it misses two years, then it is suspect. Templeton parts company from Graham on the question of growth. He is interested in financial strength and hidden asset values — very interested.

*Consistent growth is best of all.* After all, in an inflationary period just staying even in real terms means reporting growth in nominal terms. On the other hand, *one should be suspicious of hyperrapid growth. Ordinarily it is unsustainable.*

He cited Commerce Clearing House as a company with a steady growth record. I asked him about one of my own favourite financial service companies — far less established than Commerce Clearing House, to be sure, but with an extraordinary earnings growth record — H. & R. Block, then about 14. Templeton said that he expected that eventually its growth — which has been phenomenal — would be interrupted. The overhead, he thought, might eventually get out of control. I asked him about T. Rowe Price's theory that the investor should seek out the 'fertile fields for growth' in the economy — those destined to expand and flourish in the years ahead — and buy the leading companies in them. Templeton replied that at one time or another he had probably owned most of the stocks in the T. Rowe Price Growth Stock Fund, but such companies usually also have high price-earnings ratios. Quite often the specialty company is less expensive, because less understood. It takes neither training nor experience to go out and buy a highly visible premier growth stock without regard to price.

Everything has its season, which does not last forever. The world changes its spots, and the investor must change his. The T. Rowe Price big-growth stock philosophy, says Templeton, had a long day, but in the end that family of stocks became unreasonably priced. A prolongation of the earlier rate of gain could no longer be reasonably expected. The David Babson organisation in Boston, which also favoured top growth stocks, had a six-year span during which their fund almost always ran near the front of the pack. According to Templeton, by the end of that time they should have been eagerly looking for any good excuse to change their entire approach. And Morgan Guaranty, which produced such handsome results in the late 1960s and early 1970s by bidding its Avons, International Flavours, and the like to almost infinite prices — how much happier might they have been if their Mr Samuel R. Calloway had retired and they had sold the lot in 1973 — rather than in 1975, after a 50% decline.

5. *The cardinal rule is flexibility.* You must get ready to change when everything seems to be working particularly well. When the cycle is perfectly in gear with your expectations, prepare to jump.

6. *Don't trust rules and formulas.* Thirty years ago Templeton knew an officer in the trust department of the Chemical Bank who finally, after the market had puzzled so many people for countless generations, got it all together. All the numbers, all the cycles, all the psychological, financial, and fundamental data since the beginning of markets now trumpeted the same message: the Dow Jones Average was going straight down for three years. He put his clients into cash. Alas! The first year, the market went up. The second, it went up more. And the third, it went up more than ever.

Templeton's sometime partner Vance, then an elderly man, used to enjoy lecturing about investments. Part of his kit was a huge chart plotted on a roll of wrapping paper. It was so big that during his lectures he would have to get a volunteer from the audience to help him unroll it and put it on the wall. This chart plotted the market for the previous 20 years. Then there were different squiggly lines representing the various factors that influence it — industrial production, money supply, and so on. One squiggly line was best of all. It worked perfectly. Year after year if you had followed it you could have known where the market was headed and made a killing. When the audience, fascinated, demanded to know what it represented, Mr Vance told them. It was the rate his hens were laying, in the chicken coop in the back of his house.

Mr Templeton's most remarkable change of tack has come about as this book goes to the publisher.

When I first visited him in Nassau, Templeton's fund had about $20 million in assets; both he and his holdings were unrecognised. As I write this postscript, investors have jumped aboard the Templeton bandwagon: the fund is now over $200 million, and he has started a second fund which has another $70 million. He is taking in $2 million a week. You have to put that kind of money to work in big chunks, you can't seek out only tiny undervalued situations. So, Templeton, obedient to his principle of flexibility, is buying such huge names as Ford and Royal Dutch.

In this game, however, he is competing directly with the best brains in the business. Lots of people, to say the least, can figure out the investment merits of Ford and Royal Dutch. Many, on the contrary, were inhibited from following Templeton out onto the thin ice of little Canadian real estate companies and Japanese trading firms. Maybe, however, Ford and Royal Dutch really are the best bargains, regardless of the amount of money one is managing. Time will tell.

# CONTRIBUTORS

Professor Charles Birch was Professor of Biology at the University of Sydney, Australia.

Dr David G. Burke is Director of Translations Department, American Bible Society.

The Reverend Dr Charles Elliott is Dean of Trinity Hall, Cambridge, England.

Dr Thomas Gillespie is President of Princeton Theological Seminary, Princeton, New Jersey, USA.

Ms Laura Goostree is Coordinator, Major Donor Communications, American Bible Society.

The Reverend Dr Billy Graham is the noted American evangelist.

Dr Uwe Kitzinger was President of Templeton College, Oxford, England.

Mr William Simon is a former Secretary of the Treasury, USA

Sir Sigmund Sternberg is the Chairman of the Executive Committee of the International Council of Christians and Jews.

The Rt. Hon. Lord Thurlow was Governor of The Bahamas.

The Very Reverend Professor Thomas F. Torrance was Professor of Christian Dogmatics at the University of Edinburgh, Scotland.

Mr John Train is an investment manager and writer in New York.

Dr Peter Wosh is Director of Archives/Library Services, The American Bible Society.